Delight in the WORD

Col. 1: 28, 29

These reflections on life situations are skillfully written in a readable style, reflecting the practical wisdom of a pastor with a heart for God and people. Deeply rooted in Scripture, they will fortify your soul.

-LES LOFQUIST
Executive Director, IFCA International

One of the chief struggles of the modern fundamental and evangelical paradigm is the disconnect between the Holy Word of God and our lives. We are content to sit in church and hear sermons as long as we don't really have to live that way in the real world. We are comfortable to have a very high view of inspiration and simultaneously a very low view of application. Paul Tautges has struck a nerve with his very insightful work. I would call this a work in the true spirit of great practical theology. He has taken some of the immeasurable riches of the eternal Word and gotten them past our defenses and the surface levels in which we live and done radical and skillful surgery in our hearts. He has both instructed our minds and confronted our wills in his theological and yet very practical work. I can sincerely say that my delight in the unsearchable riches of the Word is much more intense after my encounter with this book. I am deeply indebted to Paul for all of his passionate study and work.

-KEVEN E. BROWNFIELD
President, Biblical Revival Ministries

Paul is a man of the Word and it flows out of him with a freshness that will encourage you greatly. You will find this work to be biblical, practical, energetic, and right where you live.

-MATTHEW OLSON
President, Northland Baptist Bible College

Delight in the WORD

40 Meditations for the Hungry Heart

Paul Tautges

Pleasant Word
A Division of WINEPRESS PUBLISHING

ISBN 1-4141-0430-8
Library of Congress Catalog Card Number: 2005902504

Dedication

To the gracious members of Immanuel Bible Church,

who first received these "letters" with joy,

teachable spirits,

and hunger for God's Word.

Thank you for the privilege of

"keeping watch over your souls with joy."

(Hebrews 13:17)

Table of Contents

Introduction

A.W. Tozer observed that, "Books are written by the scores to show that Jesus is a regular fellow and Christianity a wise use of the highest psychological laws."[1] This book is *not* one of those. Jesus is no "regular fellow," but the living Savior and Lord of repentant sinners. And biblical Christianity is not the wise integration of man-centered psychology with Scripture, but the verbal proclamation of the heart-transforming truths of God within the Gospel. It is the visual display of a life worthy of that same Gospel.

When Jesus Christ goes to work in our hearts by His grace we become *living epistles,* letters of God, known and read by men, written by "the Spirit of the living God, not on tablets of stone but on tablets of flesh, that is, of the heart" (2 Corinthians 3:2, 3). It is from this seedbed of truth that the brief articles in this volume sprout.

My goal in writing is very simple: I want to increase your love for God by increasing your delight in His Word, *The Holy Bible.* In time you will learn that the two cannot be separated for, as you will soon discover, no one can truly love God if they do not also love His Word. Jesus said, "He who has My commandments and keeps them, it is he who loves Me" (John 14:21). By demonstrating how sufficient the Scripture is in addressing the needs of the human heart, I trust that the Holy Spirit will accelerate His counseling ministry in your life and thereby lead you into a deeper, more loving obedience to God (John 16:13).

There are at least six reasons why it is spiritually profitable for us to mimic the psalmist's resolution, "I will delight myself in Your statutes; I will not forget Your word" (Psalm 119:16). Let's look at these as we begin:

- **Delighting in the Word leads to spiritual stability and fruitfulness.**

  Blessed is the man who walks not in the counsel of the ungodly, nor stands in the path of sinners, nor sits in the seat of the scornful; *but his delight is in the law of the LORD,* and in His law he meditates day and night. He shall be like a tree planted by the rivers of water, that brings forth its fruit in its season, whose leaf also shall not wither; and whatever he does shall prosper.
  (Psalm 1:1–3)

Abundant fruitfulness and oak-like stability in the Christian life are experienced in direct proportion to the extent to which we delight in God's Word. It was not merely what this man avoided (foolish and worldly counsel) that made him blessed, but what he embraced—*biblical truth.* Therefore, he who delights in the counsel of God will be blessed in all he does.

- **Delighting in the Word feeds a desire to do God's will.**

  I delight to do Your will, O my God, and Your law is within my heart.

  (Psalm 40:8)

Delighting in the will of God is tied to a commitment to the Word of God cherished in the heart. Jesus said, "For where your treasure is, there your heart will be also" (Matthew 6:21). When Jesus first taught this truth He was referring to the everyday choice of *where* we invest our wealth—in a temporal earth or an everlasting heaven. However, the principle also applies to other contexts. In other words, it is *always* true that our hearts follow our treasure. Therefore, the more we treasure God's precepts by delighting in them "more than gold" (Psalm 19:10), the greater will be our desire to obey the will of God as revealed in that Word.

- **Delighting in the Word is a cure for depression.**

  Your testimonies also are *my delight and my counselors.* My soul clings to the dust; *revive me according to Your word.*

  (Psalm 119:24, 25)

When depression strikes (or creeps in unnoticed), we need help from God. In the middle of a thick fog of depression we desperately need the piercing light of divine truth to break through with clear objectivity. So we pray: "Let Your tender mercies come to me, that I may live; *for Your law is my delight*" (Psalm 119:77). [More on this in Chapter Six.]

- **Delighting in the Word fortifies obedience to God, even when others care not.**

Teach me, O LORD, the way of Your statutes, and *I shall keep it to the end.* Give me understanding, and *I shall keep* Your law; indeed, I shall observe it with my whole heart. Make me walk in the path of Your commandments, *for I delight in it.*
(Psalm 119:33–35)

Those who truly delight in the Bible will, in turn, possess an intense desire to live in obedience to its precepts. Theirs will be a determined obedience, a steadfast adherence to truth, even in the face of opposition.

The proud have forged a lie against me, but *I will keep Your precepts* with my whole heart. Their heart is as fat as grease, but *I delight* in Your law.
(Psalm 119:69, 70)

- **Delighting in the Word nurtures a love for Scripture meditation.**

The delight of the blessed man, "is in the law of the LORD, and in His law he meditates day and night."
(Psalm 1:2)

Charles Spurgeon described this man as one who "takes a text and carries it with him all day long; and in the night watches, when sleep forsakes his eyelids, he museth upon the Word of God."[2] The more we grow in our love for God's Word, the more it will dominate our thinking about every area of our life. Then, and only then, will our minds be truly renewed, according to the promise of God (Romans 12:2).

And *I will delight* myself in Your commandments, *which I love.* My hands also I will lift up to Your commandments, *which I love,* and *I will meditate* on Your statutes.

(Psalm 119:47, 48)

• **Delighting in the Word sustains us in times of trial.**

Trouble and anguish have overtaken me, *yet Your commandments are my delights.*

(Psalm 119:143)

When the trials of life seem to drain every ounce of spiritual, physical, and emotional energy from us, God's Word will be our strength. It will minister to the deepest agony of our hearts and help us gain and keep an eternal perspective. Renewing our mind with such truths as, "the sufferings of this present time are not worthy *to be compared* with the glory which shall be revealed in us" (Romans 8:18), will compel us to agree with the Psalmist: "Unless Your law *had been my delight,* I would then have perished in *my affliction*" (Psalm 119:92).

This is just a brief sampling of what the Word of God will do for us as we make it our delight and treasure. As I compiled these articles into book form, like King Solomon of old, I "sought to find delightful words and to write words of truth correctly" (Ecclesiastes 12:10, 11 NASB). My prayer to the "One Shepherd" was that His Holy Spirit would be my guide so that you, the reader, would prosper spiritually. I trust that He has answered my prayers, at least to some small degree. If you have read this introduction through, then you are already a rare reader. *Thank you.* Now, let's delight in God's Word together!

CHAPTER ONE

Refusing to be Crippled

Thoughts on living with irreversible decisions

Irreversible decisions are the hardest to live with. You know you've done wrong, but it is too late to undo it. Now you must live with the consequences, whatever they may be. *But how?* Do you beat yourself up forever? Do you live in a state of habitual sullenness? Do you become bitter toward others or God? The pain of regret and the constant nagging of a conscience that knows it has been foolish have the potential of crippling you forever. Must this be, or is there a better way?

King David was a man forced to live with the consequences of his own irreversible poor choices. His escapade with the midnight bather (Bathsheba) was now over. He could no longer pretend it was just a bad dream. She was pregnant with his illegitimate son. Her husband was dead and the blood was on his hands—and the whole kingdom knew it. His sin was ever before him and feelings of regret had the potential of haunting him forever, leaving him spiritually incapacitated and useless to God. *But did it have to be?* Or, was there a better way?

17

Psalm 51 reveals that indeed there was a better way and David found it. It is the way of cleansing. It is the way of being washed by the forgiveness of God. It is the way of ceaseless praise for grace that is greater than sin. His musical prayer begins with a plea for grace: "Have mercy upon me, O God, according to Your lovingkindness; according to the multitude of Your tender mercies" (vs. 1). His plea to a God that he knew could only act in accordance with His character produced a bold request for pardon: "Blot out my transgressions. Wash me thoroughly from my iniquity, and cleanse me from my sin…purge me with hyssop, and I shall be clean; wash me, and I shall be whiter than snow" (vs. 2, 7).

So confident was David in the promise of God's forgiveness that he sang, "Restore to me the joy of Your salvation" (v. 12). Herein lies the secret to dismantling the crippling power of wrong choices: *we must refuse to allow the painful reality of our sin to get the upper hand by casting a dark shadow over the grace and forgiveness of God.* Satan would love for us to become so obsessed by regret that we no longer stand in awe of a God that delights in restoring hopelessly flawed sinners.

Restored to God, David was ready to be used by Him. "Then I will teach transgressors Your ways, and sinners shall be converted to You" (v. 13). Were the consequences gone? *No.* But the guilt was. Were regretful thoughts totally nonexistent? I doubt it. But David was determined to move on with God anyway. This was the Apostle Paul's choice, as well, who said: "Brethren, I do not count myself to have apprehended; but one thing I do, *forgetting those things which are behind and reaching forward* to those things which are ahead, I press toward the goal for the prize of the upward call of God in Christ Jesus" (Philippians 3:13, 14).

18

Like you, I too have made some bad yet irreversible decisions. In fact, at times I have allowed the painful consequences of these to almost overwhelm me. However, God's empowering grace has been sufficient in the end. We all have things in our past we wish we could change, but some things cannot be undone. Some can, but many cannot. Some consequences remain until the end of time, but that does not mean we must let them cripple us. Let us not become slaves to *them*, but let us make them *our* slaves, forcing us to keep the restoration of God at the forefront of our minds. Let us forbid them to hinder our growth. Let us steadfastly refuse to let them interrupt our praise. Let us give them permission to exist only as reminders of the marvelous grace of our loving Lord.

> *Sin and despair, like the sea waves cold,*
> *Threaten the soul with infinite loss;*
> *Grace that is greater, yes, grace untold,*
> *Points to the refuge, the mighty cross.*[3]

Let us not allow the effects of irreversible choices steal the joy that is found only in the refuge of the Cross of Christ!

CHAPTER TWO

A "Ten Commandments Prayer"

Based on Exodus 20:1–17

Dear Lord,
Counsel my readers by revealing the subtle deceptions of the human heart. I pray:

- **. . . that they will have no other gods before You.** *That they will not dishonor Your uniqueness. That they will not put anything or anyone in Your place, nor fall prey to the schemes of the devil by replacing the ultimate priority (You) with worldly pleasures, possessions, power, or pursuits (1 John 2:15–17). That the use of their time and energy will reflect the Lordship of Christ and that their souls will pant and thirst for You, O God, (Psalm 42:1, 2).*

- **. . . that they will not provoke Your jealousy by worshipping You through things seen, felt, or touched.** *That they will not dishonor Your nature as a Spirit being. That they will not get caught up in the elements of worship at the expense of the Person be-*

ing worshipped. That they will worship You in spirit and truth (John 4:24), and "see" You as exalted and, therefore, get caught up in "worth-ship." That they will not place their faith in human reason or things seen, but instead walk by faith, not by sight (2 Corinthians 5:7).

- **. . . that they will not use Your holy Name carelessly.** *That they will not dishonor Your character. That they will not misrepresent You by using Your Name falsely (Psalm 24:3, 4), hypocritically (Titus 1:16), blasphemously (James 2:7), rashly (Ecclesiastes 5:2, 3), or irreverently (James 3:8–11), or speak of holy things flippantly. That their talk will not be dominated by meaningless, empty or idle words (Matthew 12:36), but always by reverence and prudence.*

- **. . . that they will follow your creation principle of rest.** *That they will honor Your wisdom. That they will not allow the American "rat race" to rob them of stopping to look at the sunset (Psalm 24:1). That You will help them to be diligent and faithful workers, but at the same time guard them from becoming slaves to their earthly employments (Colossians 3:22–24). That they will not allow busyness and worldly pleasures to destroy the immense worth and uniqueness of the Lord's Day. That corporate worship will be more important than hunting, fishing, or football. That they will realize the most valuable family time is not spent in front of the TV, but in Your house learning Your Word (Acts 20:7).*

- **. . . that they will show reverence and respect for their earthly parents.** *That they will honor Your authority* structures. *That they will not be like the world—disobedient to parents (2 Timothy 3:2), but instead will teach their children to cheerfully obey, with respect. That they will not forget their elderly parents and grandparents, but will gladly accept the role reversal of becoming their caregivers (1 Timothy 5:3, 4). That they will recognize earthly parents as gifts to be honored and treasured, but not more than Christ (Matthew 10:37). That they will learn to be submissive and respectful toward the authorities You have ordained (Romans 13:1–7), while at the same time faithfully praying for their leaders (1 Timothy 2:1–4).*

- *. . .* **that they will not hate or kill.** *That they will not dishonor Your gift of life or Your love. That they will not allow the sun to go down on their anger so it becomes deep-seated hatred, resentment, or bitterness (Ephesians 4:26), or hate their brother or sister in the Lord and, therefore, be liars that dwell in darkness (1 John 2:9, 11; 3:15; 4:20). That they will love their neighbors as themselves and be lights in a dark world by cherishing the sanctity of human life, young and old and disabled. That they will show the world that children are valuable blessings, not inconveniences or burdens, and plead with You to change the hearts of women who selfishly seek abortions, men who fearfully force them, and doctors who gladly assist them.*

- *. . .* **that they will not lust or commit adultery.** *That they will not dishonor Your gift of sexuality. That husbands will rejoice in their wives and wives rejoice in their husbands (Proverbs 5:18), holding the marriage covenant in the highest regard and the marriage bed undefiled (Hebrews 13:4). That those who are unmar-*

ried will find their fullest satisfaction in You by fleeing youthful lusts and pursuing righteousness, faith, love, and peace (2 Timothy 2:22). That all would maintain purity of mind by avoiding TV programs, videos, magazines, or Internet sites that stimulate and feed the flesh (Philippians 4:8). That they will pray for the fruit of the Holy Spirit, which is self-control.

- **. . . that they will not steal from You or from others.** *That they will not dishonor Your provision. That they will not steal from You by withholding Your tithe from their church because of unbelief or self-centered spending habits (Malachi 3:8). That they will not steal from others by taking advantage of them or being habitually late for appointments. That they will flee laziness and pursue hard work (Proverbs 6:6–11), and avoid all financial dealings that put integrity into question. That they will not steal from government by cheating on their taxes (Romans 13:6), or steal from their family by wasting money on foolish habits (1 Timothy 5:8), or buy a lottery ticket or enter a casino (Proverbs 28:22). That they will learn to be good stewards of the money You have entrusted to their care, faithfully giving their firstfruits to You and wisely managing the rest.*

- **. . . that they will not lie against one another.** *That they will not dishonor Your truth. That they will not practice perjury (Proverbs 24:28), bribery (Proverbs 17:23), slander (Proverbs 10:18), gossip (Proverbs 11:13), or flattery (Psalm 12:2, 3). That they will not make false claims about themselves or wear masks to impress or deceive others, speaking only the truth in love (Ephesians 4:15), and building their relationships on trustworthiness. That they will tell the whole truth* and not reveal only the facts that make them look good. That they will be true friends by honoring confidences (Proverbs 17:9). That they will not lie in church by singing songs of worship to You from their lips and not from their hearts (Matthew 15:8). That they will honor Your truth at all times by pursuing authentic Christian living.

- **. . . that they will not crave earthly belongings.** That they will not dishonor Your gifts. That they will not desire what is not rightfully theirs and endeavor to acquire it, but instead treat other people's property with respect. That their hearts will not be captivated by affection for money or this world's goods (1 Timothy 6:8–10). That they will resist the temptation to put trust in credit cards and learn to say "no" to impulse buying. That they will replace envy with gratitude and conscious thanksgiving (1 Peter 2:1), praise instead of complain, and pray instead of worry (Philippians 4:6, 7). That they will learn to be content in any and every circumstance (Philippians 4:11).

Heavenly Father, I pray this for my readers as I pray it for myself. May You grant all of us the grace to be Your obedient servants!

In Jesus Name,
Amen.

CHAPTER THREE

Faithfulness, Pigs, and Heavenly Reward

Meditation on Colossians 3:23, 24

A s I shoveled soiled wood shavings into the wheel-barrow I meditated on the promise of God to reward His children for their faithfulness. It was the second day of the county fair and my children were responsible to be there in the wee hours of the morning to clean out their pigs' pen. As I went to wake them for their chores I realized how faithful they had been for the past five months and wanted to do something to show my love and appreciation for them. So, I let them sleep and went to do the chores by myself.

While cleaning, I occasionally glanced at the ribbons they had received the day before, remembering that none of their five pigs had placed high enough to make it to every young pig-raiser's dream—the meat animal auction. There they had the potential of earning many times more than their initial investment of stock, feed, and time. I found myself thinking, "But, Lord, all summer long, I told my kids You are the Rewarder of faithfulness. I even quoted Proverbs to them about the rewards of diligent work. They were so

25

faithful. I don't understand why You did not reward them."
In my thoughts I heard Him answer.

*"My son, I do reward faithfulness, but I never promised
that the reward would always be earthly."*

I immediately felt as though I had had an old truth re-
taught to me in a whole new way. A few hours later, at the
breakfast table, I shared my discovery with my family. I told
them how the Lord had counseled me with His Word and
given me fresh insight into the whole area of faithfulness,
then shared with them the principles of Colossians 3:23,
24: "And whatever you do, do it heartily, as to the Lord
and not to men, knowing that from the Lord you will receive the reward of the inheritance; for you serve the Lord
Christ." How often I had quoted the first verse without the
second and missed the promise of future reward! If we are
truly working for the Lord rather than for men how ironic
it is that we look to this world for our reward. With those
thoughts ringing clear, I proceeded to teach the following
principles:

• **Faithfulness should be the practice of our lives, with
  or without earthly reward.**

  We need to cultivate faithfulness simply because it
  is the right thing to do; it is one of the marks of wise
  stewardship. "Moreover it is required in stewards that
  one be found *faithful*" (1 Corinthians 4:2). Believers
  should be known for their faithfulness. The Apostle
  Paul addressed the saints in Ephesus as those who were
  "*faithful* in Christ Jesus" (Ephesians 1:1), and called the
  Colossian believers "*faithful brethren* in Christ"
  (Colossians 1:1, 2).

- **God** *always* **rewards faithfulness, but not always in** *this* **life.**

  We need to cultivate faithfulness with confidence and contentment in the knowledge that, even if we are never noticed or rewarded on earth, we will one day receive a heavenly reward. We must be diligent in our service for God, "knowing that from the Lord [we] will receive the reward of the inheritance." The very word "inheritance" is jam-packed with future outlook. Jesus instilled this kind of focus into His disciples in order to produce perseverance. "Blessed are you when men hate you, and when they exclude you, and revile you, and cast out your name as evil, for the Son of Man's sake. Rejoice in that day and leap for joy! *For indeed your reward is great in heaven,* for in like manner their fathers did to the prophets" (Luke 6:22, 23). Looking for our heavenly reward is a legitimate motivation toward greater faithfulness in this life.

So, as we seek to glorify God in every aspect of our lives, may we remember that His promise of reward will not always be fully realized in this life, but certainly in the life to come. Let us faithfully press on to obtain the heavenly reward!

CHAPTER FOUR

A Counselor Named Grace

The power of the Gospel and an
"Extraordinary Savior"

The church of Jesus Christ once believed His words:
"And you shall know the truth, and the truth shall
make you free" (John 8:32). Unfortunately, things
have changed. Today, Christian preachers and authors
too numerous to count subtly deny this once-cherished,
commonly-held belief. Now, instead of the simple Gospel
breaking the chains of sin, people need an endless variety of
twelve-step programs to overcome every conceivable malady
of the soul—or specifically worded prayers to "tear down
demonic strongholds." The sad reality is that the church that
once believed God's Word had the power to pierce the heart,
soul, and mind now has more confidence in psychological
counseling, therapy, and medication.

You can see then why I was so pleased to reread a little
book I was introduced to almost a decade ago, called simply *Glenda's Story*.[4] It is just that: one woman's humble
testimony of the transforming grace of God contained in
the Gospel. Glenda's mentor, Elisabeth Elliot, writes in the
foreword:

Abandonment, abortion, abuse, addiction, adultery, alcoholism, alienation, anorexia—words hardly understood a few generations ago but now on everyone's tongue, words we can hardly escape if we pick up a newspaper or turn on the television. It is generally taken for granted that these sins and sorrows can be dealt with only by law, or by something we heard little about years ago—counseling. The results of such measures are not always brilliant.

Glenda's story, comprising all of those "A" words, reveals the wondrous efficacy of a far older answer, an answer far less frequently sought today, except as a desperate venture—the Cross of Jesus....Glenda, just a little girl, had no idea that her sufferings were common. She carried the heavy baggage of guilt and fear, had never heard of counseling, and would not have known where to turn if she had. Her story, horrifying proof of the reality of sin and of the perils of living in a broken world, carries us up and out into the radiance of a loving Father who knew her heart, saw her tears, and through His amazing grace led her to that old, rugged Cross, of which is said what cannot be said of anything else in the world—"it is the power of God for the salvation of everyone who believes" (pp. 13, 14).

Far from being a "woe-is-me-for-all-I've-been-through" kind of story, Glenda Revell writes in the preface of her autobiography: "If this were just a story about my suffering, it would be ordinary, for suffering is as commonplace as life itself. Rather, this is my account of an extraordinary Savior, who brings light out of darkness, joy out of sorrow, peace out of pain" (p. 15). And what a refreshing account it is! What is so refreshing about this little book is that there exists not even the slightest hint of thought or feeling of victimization. Not that there is no such thing as a victim, but when God's grace fills a sinner's heart the *victim*

29

mentality fades because suffering is understood as a sinner's lot in life and, even more importantly, a tool in the hands of a wise and loving God to draw us to the Savior. This in no way minimizes the reality of wickedness or makes God the cause of it. Sexual abuse is all-too-real and is incredibly damaging to the soul. As a pastor who has counseled the violated, I know. But the good news is that where sin abounds, God's grace abounds all the more. It is grace that can take a violated girl and turn her into a woman with this kind of perspective:

> Today it is fashionable, almost desirable, to be a victim. Everyone has a story, and no one can be outdone when it comes to how severely he has been abused. Even in Christian circles this is a popular theme. The attitude that dominates these tales of woe is, "Someone has violated me and intruded on my rights. Having endured this commends me, makes me special to God. He is now, or will, or should be giving me the peace, happiness, contentment and success that were rightfully mine all along." Such thinking is seriously flawed because it is based on the false supposition that humans are innately good and therefore deserving of only the best life has to offer. (p. 33)

That last sentence is worth repeating: "Such thinking is seriously flawed because it is based on the false supposition that humans are innately good and therefore deserving of only the best life has to offer." What flaw in thinking is she referring to? It is the flaw of thinking more highly of ourselves than we ought to think; it is the idea that we are entitled to special treatment from God *because* of being abused. The irony of it all is that this attitude of self-pity actually becomes a barrier to true inner healing. Those who feel this way cannot be fully delivered by God because they are so focused on the wrongs committed against themselves by others that they cannot see their own desperate need of redemption. Grace cannot help us as long as we think we deserve better treatment than we have received. Grace comes to our rescue when we accept numerous injustices as God's means of drawing us to Himself. This is the renewal of mind Glenda experienced, as evidenced by her testimony:

> I have heard people ask, "How can God be loving and kind when He allows such suffering in the lives of innocent children?" The answer lies in perspective. As any loving parent knows, he must sometimes withhold seemingly good things for the ultimate good of his child.
>
> Likewise, our dear Father is much more concerned with our eternal destiny than with giving us temporal pleasure. And unlike earthly fathers, God knows precisely what we need of both pain and pleasure to draw us to the ultimate good He has planned for us.
>
> I know now that God did not forsake me during my dark night of sorrow. All the time He was drawing me to Himself by peeling away, one by one, those objects of my longing that, if given, would have kept me from longing for Him. God was on my side. His strong arm, which in His great wisdom so sorely bruised me, would eventually, in merciful tenderness, gather me into His bosom. (pp. 61, 62)

The good news of the biblical Gospel is that grace abounds over our sins *and* the sins committed against us because Jesus endured the ultimate abuse, and it is through self-abandoning faith in Him that we are made free. This is the truth that converted Saul, the abuser, into Paul, the apostle. Hear his words:

31

And I thank Christ Jesus our Lord who has enabled me, because He counted me faithful, putting me into the ministry, although I was formerly a blasphemer, a persecutor, and an insolent man; but I obtained mercy because I did it ignorantly in unbelief. And *the grace of our Lord was exceedingly abundant,* with faith and love which are in Christ Jesus.

(1 Timothy 1:12–14)

Of Paul's description of his past, William MacDonald writes, "Although it is not as obvious from the English words, there is an ascending scale of wickedness in the three words blasphemer, persecutor, and insolent man [violent aggressor]. The first sin is a matter of words only. The second describes *suffering inflicted on others* for their religious beliefs. The third includes the idea of cruelty and abuse."[5] It is from *these* sins that grace rescued Paul. This is the grace that leads us to experience the freedom that comes from being forgiven by God and to decide to forgive those who have sinned against us. But this road must be *chosen.* Ed Bulkley has well said, "You can choose to remain a victim the rest of your life, or you can choose the path of victory by following One who was abused as no other."[6]

Dear friend, if you or someone you love has been scarred by any one of the many faces of abuse, run as fast as you can into the arms of a counselor named "grace." God is the only true Healer of our souls and His prescribed medicine is the Cross of Jesus. In Him alone, grace is more than abundant to overcome all our sins and mercy is plentiful to heal all our wounds. In the words of the old hymn, this transforming truth is powerfully proclaimed:

In the old rugged cross, stained with blood so divine;
A wondrous beauty I see; for 'twas on that old cross
Jesus suffered and died to pardon and sanctify me.

So I'll cherish the old rugged cross, till my trophies at last I lay down.
I will cling to the old rugged cross, and exchange it someday for a crown.[7]

Glory in the Cross and in the Cross alone!

CHAPTER FIVE

The Heart of the Matter

Where true change begins . . .

In our culture the heart has become symbolic of one's affections. Though the word *heart* is used on occasion in an emotional sense in the Bible, that is not its primary meaning. Since God's Word intentionally addresses the issues of our heart, it is crucial that we understand just what the Bible means by this term. Three key teachings within Scripture come to mind:

- **The heart is the "control center" of life.**

  When the Bible speaks of the heart it is not referring to the blood-pumping organ in our chest or the fluttering of emotions, but rather the whole inner man—*mind, emotions,* and *will*. Solomon instructed his son to keep his heart "with all diligence, for out of it spring the issues of life" (Proverbs 4:23). The computer I am using is a wonderful machine, yet it does not work without an operator. As much as I wish, it does not sit on my desk working diligently while I am at home sleeping.

Just as I must command it to do what I want it to do, so our heart is the *command center* of our lives. No wonder God tells us to guard our hearts!

In the Sermon on the Mount, Jesus instructed His disciples and the listening multitude to be careful where they directed their affections. He said:

> Do not lay up for yourselves treasures on the earth, where moth and rust destroy and where thieves break in and steal; but lay up for yourselves treasures in heaven, where neither moth nor rust destroys and where thieves do not break in and steal. For where your treasure is, there will your heart be also.
> (Matthew 6:19–21)

What we highly treasure and consider important will affect every area of our lives. To put it another way, "what we worship is what we will serve." In other words, the heart of the matter *is* the heart.

- **The heart is by nature deceitful and wicked.**

The prophet Jeremiah wrote: "the heart is deceitful above all things, and desperately wicked; who can know it?" (Jeremiah 17:9). By nature our inner man does not crave the things that please God. Instead it demands its own wicked inclinations be served immediately. Thankfully, God has promised to provide us a way of escape when the temptations of our hearts compel us to deny God and exalt self:

> No temptation has overtaken you except such as is common to man; but God is faithful, who will not allow you to be tempted beyond what you are able,

35

but with the temptation will also make the way of escape, that you may be able to bear it.

(1 Corinthians 10:13)

- **God gives us a new heart at the moment of salvation.**

Though the control center of our lives is utterly depraved, God's Word gives believers great hope. It assures us that, at the moment of saving faith, God gives us a new heart. He makes us partakers of the divine nature (2 Peter 1:4), thus enabling us to please Him. The Apostle Paul wrote to the Corinthian Church: "Therefore if anyone is in Christ, he is a new creation; old things have passed away; behold, all things have become new" (2 Corinthians 5:17). Does this mean that the old nature is eradicated and sin is something we no longer deal with? *Absolutely not!* How, then, do we submit to the power of this new heart?

First, we must be walking in the Spirit. When this is the case, we will not fulfill the lusts of the flesh, our old heart (Galatians 5:16). To walk in the Spirit is to walk according to the book He wrote—the Bible. Resisting the influence of our flesh is a constant battle that can only be successfully fought with the aid of the indwelling Spirit of God *as we submit* our will to the authority of Scripture. In other words, you cannot separate these two responsibilities. To walk in the Spirit is equal to walking according to the Book He inspired. The instructions following the command to be filled (controlled) by the Spirit (Ephesians 5:15–33) are virtually the same as those that follow the command to be filled with the Word of God (Colossians 3:16–25).

36

Only the Word of God empowered by the Holy Spirit has the power to perform the heart surgery we need (Hebrews 4:12). If we want to see transformation in our own lives and help others experience biblical change, we must allow God's Word to get to the heart of the matter.

CHAPTER SIX

Working through Depression

Meditation on Psalm 119:25–32

"My soul clings to the dust; revive me according to Your word. I have declared my ways, and You answered me; teach me Your statutes. Make me understand the way of Your precepts; so shall I meditate on Your wonderful works. My soul melts from heaviness; strengthen me according to Your word. Remove from me the way of lying, and grant me Your law graciously. I have chosen the way of truth; Your judgments I have laid before me. I cling to Your testimonies; O LORD, do not put me to shame! I will run the course of Your commandments, for You shall enlarge my heart."

—Psalm 119:25–32

Depression is debilitating. It is a crippling state that leaves you unable to function normally and, sometimes, not even caring that it is so. You may feel sad. You may feel angry. You may not feel at all. You may simply be *numb*.

It may surprise you to know that the man who wrote the greatest poem exalting the beauties of the Word of God, Psalm 119, battled depression. So depressed was he that he said, "My soul clings to the dust" (v. 25), but just eight verses later he was able to shout, "I will run the course of Your commandments, for You shall enlarge my heart" (v. 32). How did he get from laying in the dirt to running in the race?

I hope to encourage you by showing how he worked *through* depression. That, I believe, is the key. When you are depressed, you sometimes just want to sit and wait for it to go away, but it rarely resolves *itself*, unless it is simply a long nap that you need. The most difficult part of being depressed is that you must continue to live. *But how?* How do you go on with your life? How do you go to work tomorrow? How will you get out of bed? The answer is: you must begin to take *small steps* of action through the fog. Three clues as to how to do this are given in Psalm 119:

1. Identify the Cause of Your Depression. (vv. 25–29)

First, you must discern what it is that has led you to this point.

- Begin with prayer. (v. 25)
  Notice that immediately after his admission of depression: "My soul clings to the dust," David cried out to God: "Revive me according to Your word." God must be the one you run to first when you are depressed. If you do not know what to say to Him, pray something like this: "For [my] soul is bowed down to the dust; [my] body clings to the ground. Arise for [my] help, and redeem [me] for Your mercies' sake" (Psalm 44:25, 26).

- Evaluate your life. (v. 26)
  The next thing David did was examine his life with God's help. "I have declared my ways, and You

answered me; teach me Your statutes." As he re-
hearsed his heart attitudes and actions before God,
the Holy Spirit gave him insight into the potential
causes of his depression. This resulted in a renewed
desire to learn more of God's truth.

- Plead for understanding. (v. 27)
  "Make me understand the way of Your precepts;
  so shall I meditate on Your wonderful works." It is
  impossible to see through the dark clouds of depression without the light of God's truth. Meditate on the
  wonderful works of God displayed on the pages of
  Scripture, which bring understanding and hope.

- Admit you have no strength. (v. 28)
  Sometimes when you are depressed you may find it
  hard to admit just how helpless you really are, but
  that is pride. Admit your weakness to God; He is
  already aware of it. "My soul melts from heaviness;
  strengthen me according to Your word." Humble
  yourself before Him and seek encouragement from
  His Word.

- Confess sin and be cleansed. (v. 29)
  It appears God answered this man's prayer for understanding by exposing his sin of dishonesty. "Remove
  from me the way of lying, and grant me Your law
  graciously." Sometimes depression is the result of
  sin, and the saddened state is evidence of the Holy
  Spirit's conviction and grief. It may also be the tool
  God uses to put His finger on something specific in
  your heart or life that you may be blind to. When
  this occurs, honest confession cleanses and puts you
  back on the road to rehabilitation.

2. Decide to Let God Rehabilitate You. (vv. 30, 31)

Second, you must make a conscious choice to follow God's remedy.

- Choose to follow God's Word. (v. 30)
  In order to reap the benefits of God's rehabilitation program you must make a decision to obey God by being a *doer* of the Word and not a *hearer only* (James 1:22). "I have chosen the way of truth; Your judgments I have laid before me." This man made such encouraging progress because he was serious about delighting in Scripture. If God has revealed areas of disobedience that may be contributing to your depression, you need to consciously turn away from those false ways toward the way of truth. "Happy is he who keeps the law" (Proverbs 29:18).

- Cling to God's Word as your source of hope. (v. 31)
  When you are depressed, hope seems impossibly far away. That is the time to completely bypass feelings and, like a child, simply believe what God's Word says. The Bible is the only reliable, rock-solid source of hope. Hang on to simple truth, even if you feel it is by your fingernails, most of which are already bitten off! "I cling to Your testimonies; O LORD, do not put me to shame!"

3. Rededicate Yourself to a Life of Obedience. (v. 32)

Thirdly, when God renews your spirit through His life-giving Word, recommit yourself to living a life of faith, trust, and obedience—a life pleasing to Him. Whether your depression was caused by sin or by something else, the time is always appropriate to say to the Lord, "I will run the course of Your commandments, for You shall enlarge my heart."

CHAPTER SEVEN

Woe, Woe, Woe, Woe, Woe, Feelings

The importance of believing before we feel

Too often we worship at the throne of our feelings. We are far more prone to say, "This is how I *feel,* therefore, I will do . . .," rather than, "this is what I *think,* because the Bible says . . ." Today's emotion-driven Christianity desperately needs the wisdom of this prayer from the Puritan age:

> *Lord,*
> *Help me to honor Thee by believing before I feel,*
> *for great is the sin if I make a feeling a cause of faith.*[8]

Stop! Go back and read that again. The only proper ground of faith is the never-changing, always-enduring Word of God. Take the eleventh chapter of Hebrews, the "faith chapter," for example. Notice the relationship of God's Word to faith; i.e., how biblical faith is a response to God's objective revelation, rather than the result of something we *feel:*

By faith Noah, being divinely *warned of things* not yet seen, moved with godly fear, prepared an ark for the saving of his household, by which he condemned the world and became heir of the righteousness which is according to faith.

By faith Abraham obeyed *when he was called* to go out to the place which he would receive as an inheritance. And he went out, not knowing where he was going.

By faith Sarah herself also received strength to conceive seed, and she bore a child when she was past the age, *because she judged Him faithful who had promised.*
(Hebrews 11:7, 8, 11)

Do you see the pattern? These heroes of faith believed *before* they felt. If the opposite had been true, we can be assured they would not be members of the Hall of Faith. If Noah had waited until he *felt* like building a large boat, having never seen rain, he would've never driven the first peg. If Abraham had waited until he *felt* like leaving his parents to obey God's call, he would've died of old age in his father's house. If Sarah had waited until she *felt* like believing that a ninety-year-old woman could have a baby, she would still be laughing. What makes these people stand out is their act of obeying God's revelation even if (especially if) their feelings did not agree. That is biblical faith!

What is so desperately needed among Christians today is a return to the Word of God as the *objective standard of truth* and the final authority of "what God said" and, therefore, what we must believe and act upon. Far too often we hear things like, "I just know this is God's will; it just *feels* right," when any objective person looking in from the outside can clearly see it is not possible. God has "made an eternal covenant with His Word." He will not break it because *He* is true and His Word (His mind in written form) is Truth. He will never lead His children contrary to its clear teachings or general principles—even when our feelings convince us otherwise.

I am not advocating a denial of emotions, for it is God who created us as emotional beings; rather, I am calling us to return emotions to their proper place—as *responders* to truth, not judges of it. Douglas Wilson says it well:

> The Bible does not speak of subordinating the emotions to reason, as the rationalists desire, or even of subordinating reason to the emotions, as the romantics want. Rather, the whole man—body, soul, spirit—should be subordinated to the Word of God. The greatest commandment...requires that we love God with all our heart, soul, mind, and strength (Deuteronomy 6:4–9). In other words, reason and emotion should stop squabbling like cantankerous siblings and learn to obey their parents directly. Reason must submit to Scripture. The emotions must be brought under the authority of Scripture. And it is the task of true education to see that both do so.[9]

This is what we need. When this is *not* the habit of our lives, as the Puritans well knew, "great is the sin if [we] make a feeling a cause of faith.

CHAPTER EIGHT

An Antidote to Envy

The power of thanksgiving

As I was thinking about the Thanksgiving season it occurred to me that one of the chief obstacles preventing our growth toward becoming truly thankful is envy.

Webster's defines envy as, "a feeling of discontent and ill-will because of another's advantages." *Vine's Expository Dictionary of Old and New Testament Words* says *phthonos* (translated "envy") means, "the feeling of displeasure produced by witnessing or hearing of the advantage or prosperity of others; this evil sense always attaches to this word."[10]

Biblically speaking, envy is the product of a depraved mind (Romans 1:28, 29), a fruit of the flesh (Galatians 5:19–21), and a sin we must actively put off (1 Peter 2:1–3). If envy is a regular part of our life, it is evidence of walking in the flesh not the Spirit, and it will hinder our spiritual growth.

CAUSES OF ENVY

The New Testament exposes at least four causes of envy:

- *First*, an ungrateful heart is perfectly fertilized for the seeds of envy to take root (Romans 1:21, 29). When we allow this to happen, others' lives appear better than ours. All of a sudden everyone else is happier, richer, better looking, and more suitably situated in life. If this emotion is not nipped in the bud, we become slaves to comparison.

- *Second*, pride, cloaking itself in selfish ambition, is the perfect breeding ground for envy (Philippians 1:7; James 3:14). Selfish ambition is the drive to be better than others. It is this quest for preeminence that drives materialism. The late Ray Stedman wrote, "People really do not want things; they want to be admired for the things they have. What they want is not the new car itself, but to hear the neighbors say, 'How lucky you are to have such a beautiful car!' That is what people want—to be the center, the focus of attention."[11] We must examine our motives, because as long as we are energized by the boastful pride of life our hearts will be filled with envy toward those who "steal our glory."

- *Third*, envy demonstrates a lack of biblical love. The "love chapter" states that *love does not envy* (1 Corinthians 13:4). It is impossible to love and envy at the same time, because envy is self-focused, while love is others-focused. When we are obeying God's command to *walk in love* (Ephesians

47

5:2) we will consider others more important than ourselves.

- *Fourth,* those who have a "debate mentality" often struggle with the sin of envy. Paul described the conceited false teacher in Ephesus as one who "is obsessed with disputes and arguments over words, *from which come envy*" (1 Timothy 6:4). This is a picture of a person filled with spiritual pride, a Pharisee who needs to be recognized as the most spiritual person and, therefore, one who envies those that truly possess what he masquerades to have.

NEGATIVE RESULTS OF ENVY

The Bible recognizes at least four destructive consequences of envy:

- *First,* envy often results in broken relationships. Since the fruit of the Spirit is primarily *relational,* Paul instructed the Galatians, "If we live in the Spirit, let us also walk in the Spirit. Let us not become conceited, provoking one another, envying one another" (Galatians 5:25, 26).
- *Second,* envy often results in delivering up one's perceived enemies. If the envious person cannot "top" those he is consumed with, he may resort to betrayal. Both Matthew and Mark inform us that Jesus, "knew that they [chief priests and elders] had handed Him over because of envy" (Matthew 27:18; Mark 15:10).
- *Third,* envy may even end up causing health problems. Proverbs 14:30 says, "A sound heart is life to the body, but envy is rottenness to the bones."

- *Fourth,* envy can have a snowball effect leading to other sins. "But as for me, my feet had almost stumbled; my steps had nearly slipped. For I was envious of the boastful, when I saw the prosperity of the wicked" (Psalm 73:2, 3). Envy and covetousness walk hand in hand.

PREVENTING ENVY

Here are three steps of *preventative maintenance* for every believer. By applying this counsel, we will rid our lives of any envious attitude that may already exist and guard our hearts from its subtle intrusion, thus avoiding its tragic consequences.

1. **Nuture a thankful heart.**
   Envy feeds off of ingratitude. Therefore, in order to deal with envy we must learn to be thankful. First Thessalonians 5:18 says, "in everything give thanks." Instead of envying another person's gifts or abilities, the believer should think of all the reasons why he should be thankful for that person. Sinful thought patterns must be replaced with godly ones so that, in turn, the "reasons" to envy another person are turned into reasons to thank God for them. For example, if Bob envies Mark, then Bob should make a list of the qualities in Mark for which he can be thankful and then commit himself to thanking God every time Mark comes to mind. Giving thanks to God in prayer guards the heart from anxiety and fills it with His peace (Philippians 4:6).

2. **Nurture a content heart.**
   Guarding our hearts from envy also includes *cultivating contentment.* We must remember: God wants His

children to be content with the most basic provisions of life, "having food and clothing, with these we shall be content" (1 Timothy 6:8). Paul's own testimony is that he had "learned in whatever state I am, to be content" (Philippians 4:11). Contentment is being satisfied with what God has given us. To nurture contentment, make a list of all the blessings you now enjoy that are above the bare necessities of food and protection. This list could then be used as a guide in your personal praise time with God.

3. **Nurture a rejoicing heart.**
    We must also learn to rejoice with other believers when their blessings seem to exceed our own. Here is where the utter selfishness of envy is revealed. Envy is selfish because it leads to wallowing in self-pity thus preventing us from truly rejoicing when others' lives are blessed. Through self-discipline we must strive to replace these selfish feelings of displeasure with those of rejoicing so that we can indeed "rejoice in the Lord always" (Philippians 4:4), and "rejoice with those who rejoice" (Romans 12:15).

As people who are actively engaged in a battle against the flesh, we must recognize the base nature of envy and actively put it aside. As we learn to nurture thankful, content, and rejoicing hearts, the *peace* of God will fill us and the *joy* of the Lord will be our strength.

CHAPTER NINE

Red and Yellow, Black and White

America is looking more and more like heaven

On Sunday, December 23, 2001, our local paper ran a front-page article on the growing racial diversity of our state. It said:

Thread by thread, the predominantly white fabric of Northeastern Wisconsin took on more color in the 1990s... the number of nonwhites in the 2000 census is nearly double that of the 1990 census. And while local experts say the growth has been a plus, they hint that the diversity isn't always embraced. However, J. Allen Johnson, founding director of the Multicultural Center of Greater Green Bay, says, "from my perspective, we are a multicultural community. That is a fact. We are a multicultural region. That is a fact."

This is remarkable, considering that Sheboygan, Wisconsin, was once a "closed community" in which nonwhites were not welcome—and it was not too far back in our past! This obvious change in the makeup of our region should compel us to ask whether or not we are ready and willing and even *eager* to become a multi-ethnic church. After all, heaven itself will be a racially diverse place. When the Apostle John received the Revelation, he got a glimpse of the throne room of God. There he saw twenty-eight beings worshipping God: "And they sang a new song, saying: 'You are worthy to take the scroll, and to open its seals; for You were slain, and have redeemed us to God by Your blood out of every tribe and tongue and people and nation'" (Revelation 5:9).

The Word of God makes it very clear that God will one day receive worship from every ethnic group. "All nations whom You have made shall come and worship before You, O Lord, and shall glorify Your name" (Psalm 86:9).

Scripture also indicates that during the time of the Tribulation an angel will fly in mid-heaven, "having the everlasting Gospel to preach to those who dwell on the earth—to every nation, tribe, tongue, and people" (Revelation 14:6). This preaching is patterned after the multi-ethnicity of our missionary mandate to:

- ...make disciples of *all nations.* (Matthew 28:19)
- ...preach the Gospel to *every creature.* (Mark 16:15)
- ...declare His glory among the nations, His wonders among *all peoples.* (Psalm 96:3)

This past spring our church leadership team was approached by a small group of Hispanic people looking for a facility in which to conduct Spanish-speaking services. Wisdom led us to reject the request due to lack of doctrinal unity, but the idea did not die there. Instead it led us to commit to asking the Lord to develop our church in new ways so that one day we might have a more effective ministry to our diversified community. We are not alone. Others in the congregation are becoming alert to our need to become more intentional in our ministry to other ethnic groups. Thanks to one family's thoughtful gift, we now have Bibles available for guests who read and speak Hmong or Spanish.

I remember how startled I was the first time I heard a believer in Christ make comments that were racially derogative. I was a relatively new believer, so I was not armed with corrective Bible verses. However, in light of the biblical picture of heaven and our all-encompassing mandate for preaching, I believe I can now say with Scriptural authority that racial prejudice is sin. If God is presently in the process of calling individuals from every nation, tribe, and tongue, how can His people reflect otherwise? As the beloved children's song goes:

> Jesus loves the little children, all the children of the world.
> Red and yellow, black and white, they are precious in His sight.
> Jesus loves the little [and big] children of the world!

As our community becomes increasingly multi-ethnic, we are forced to ask ourselves if we really believe the message of that song. Will you join me in praying that the Lord will make our churches into closer reflections of heaven?

CHAPTER TEN

How Martin Burnham Gained Life by Losing It

*Bible promises that became reality
on June 7, 2002*

On June 7, 2002, a forty-two-year-old man gained his life when he was shot to death in the Philippines. Soldiers attempted to rescue missionaries Martin and Gracia Burnham 376 days after their capture. As a result, Martin, as well as a nurse who had been held hostage with them, was killed. Gracia was injured, but freed, and has been reunited with her three children in Kansas. This surprising end to a yearlong struggle motivated me to meditate anew on the commitments embraced by radical discipleship. As a result, I have discovered several principles yielding promise of eternal reward. I have written these thoughts down so we may not miss one of those prime "teaching moments" God so often provides for our growth.

[A tip for parents: use this as a guide in leading your family in a discussion of what it means to follow Christ to the end. Then spend time praying together for the families of Christian martyrs and the spread of the Gospel in dangerous lands. You may also want to read out loud Gracia's own story, *In the Presence of My Enemies.*[12]]

1. **Matthew 10:37–39**: "He who loves father or mother more than Me is not worthy of Me. And he who loves son or daughter more than Me is not worthy of Me. And he who does not take his cross and follow after Me is not worthy of Me. He who finds his life will lose it, and he who loses his life for My sake will find it."

    - **Principle**: Loyalty to Christ is of greater importance than earthly family.
    - **Promise**: He who gives up all for the sake of Christ will find true fulfillment.
    - **Martin's reward**: He found his life and became worthy of Christ.

2. **John 12:24, 25**: "Most assuredly, I say to you, unless a grain of wheat falls into the ground and dies, it remains alone; but if it dies, it produces much grain. He who loves his life will lose it, and he who hates his life in this world will keep it for eternal life."

    - **Principle**: Death to self is the path to greater fruitfulness.
    - **Promise**: Death experienced because of the work of the Gospel will never be wasted.
    - **Martin's reward**: His life commitment will become a seed bearing fruit for the cause of world missions.

3. **Philippians 1:19–23**: "For I know that this will turn out for my deliverance through your prayer and the supply of the Spirit of Jesus Christ, according to my earnest expectation and hope that in nothing I shall be

ashamed, but with all boldness, as always, so now also Christ will be magnified in my body, whether by life or by death. For to me, to live is Christ, and to die is gain. But if I live on in the flesh, this will mean fruit from my labor; yet what I shall choose I cannot tell. For I am hard-pressed between the two, having a desire to depart and be with Christ, which is far better."

- **Principle:** Christ is exalted in the life and death of those surrendered to Him.
- **Promise:** Death for the believer will be greater gain than anything this world offers.
- **Martin's reward:** Christ is presently being exalted through the death of Martin's body and Martin's gain is greater than his loss.

4. **Revelation 2:10:** "Do not fear any of those things which you are about to suffer. Indeed, the devil is about to throw some of you into prison, that you may be tested, and you will have tribulation ten days. Be faithful until death, and I will give you the crown of life."

- **Principle:** Believers need not fear suffering or death.
- **Promise:** Believers who remain faithful until death will be rewarded.
- **Martin's reward:** He is presently wearing the "crown of life."

5. **1 Corinthians 13:3:** "And though I bestow all my goods to feed the poor, and though I give my body to be burned, but have not love, it profits me nothing."

- **Principle:** Death for the sake of death is worthless. Death for the sake of the love of Christ is of great value.
- **Promise:** Selfless ministry motivated by love will lead to eternal profit.
- **Martin's reward:** His love for Christ and the lost people of the Philippines has brought him great profit.

6. **2 Corinthians 5:8–10:** "We are confident, yes, well-pleased rather to be absent from the body and to be present with the Lord. Therefore we make it our aim, whether present or absent, to be well-pleasing to Him. For we must all appear before the judgment seat of Christ, that each one may receive the things done in the body, according to what he has done, whether good or bad."

- **Principle:** It is preferable to be absent from the body and at home with the Lord.
- **Promise:** Death immediately ushers the believer into the Presence of God, where he will be compensated for his deeds.
- **Martin's reward:** At this very moment he is experiencing the supreme pleasure of eternal, never-ending, sin-free, fellowship with God. Think of it!

A biblical perspective forbids us to view the death of a believer the same way as someone who does not know God since we do not grieve, "as others who have no hope" (1 Thessalonians 4:13). We grieve with the families who suffer immediate loss—"we weep with those who weep," but we also, "rejoice with those who rejoice"

57

(Romans 12:15) because the truth of God's Word fills us with undying hope.

May God grant us grace to learn from the faithful example of those who have gone before us. May their courage spur us on to a deeper commitment to radical, Christ-like discipleship. May we be brought to the point where we really believe that "to live is Christ, and to die is gain" (Philippians 1:21).

CHAPTER ELEVEN

You Can Become "Competent to Counsel"

The rediscovery of biblical counseling

I am thrilled to be a witness of the rediscovery of biblical counseling! "Now in order to rediscover something, it must have been lost,"[13] says David Powlison. Unfortunately, that is true. Powlison explains:

> In the nineteenth and twentieth centuries, American Christians basically lost the use of truths and skills they formerly possessed. That is, practical wisdom in the cure of souls waned…. The Church lost that crucial component of pastoral skill that can be called case-wisdom—wisdom that knows people, knows how people change, and knows how to help people change.[14]

As a result, Christians sprinkled man-centered psychology with a few Bible verses and called it "Christian psychology." The outcome has been confusion, hopelessness, and the abandonment of biblical faith. John MacArthur is right when he says Christian psychology "has diminished the Church's confidence in Scripture, prayer, fellowship, and preaching as means through which the Spirit of God works to change lives."[15] It is sad to think that God's Church could lose something so basic and essential as the skill and conviction to use Scripture to help people work through their problems. Yet that is where the American church is. Those who embrace psychology as the answer are in the majority by far. There is no reason to pretend they are not. But to know that God is, in our lifetime, calling His people back to His Word as a working manual for life is exciting to say the least. This is what is referred to as *biblical counseling.*

Biblical counseling is built on the premise that God's "divine power has given to us all things that pertain to life and godliness" (2 Peter 1:3). This was the conviction of the early Christians. They had the godly audacity to believe that man can become complete in Christ without the help of psychologists, psychiatrists, or mood-altering drugs. They believed this because of three basic presuppositions that grew out of their study of the Scriptures. These are that:

1. **God's Word is sufficient to deal with every problem man faces.**

   In our day pastors are intimidated by the mental health "professionals," but the early Christians believed there is nothing man experiences that God does not directly or indirectly address in His Word. They believed that the Scriptures are sufficient to teach us doctrine—truth with a capital T. They believed that the Word confronts us when we get off the right path and then shows us how to get back on it. And they believed that the Scriptures train us to live godly lives so we mature and become equipped to serve God. In short, they believed that:

> All Scripture is given by inspiration of God, and is profitable for doctrine, for reproof, for correction, for instruction in righteousness, that the man of God may be complete, thoroughly equipped for every good work.
>
> (2 Timothy 3:16, 17)

2. Man is responsible for his own actions.

Today blame-shifting has almost become a virtue; everyone is a "victim." But the early Christians had the courage to lay fault at the right doorstep. We often read of people like the fifty-six-year-old man who sued four major fast food chains because of health problems caused by his obesity. Of course, *he* is not responsible for putting his hand to his mouth. It is the restaurant's fault! This man is consoled in our society. However, in biblical times he would have received a sermon on gluttony. How refreshing it is when the light of truth pierces so sharply through the thick cloud of man's deception! One particular Scripture comes to mind:

> Let no one say when he is tempted, 'I am tempted by God'; for God cannot be tempted by evil, nor does He Himself tempt anyone. But each one is tempted when he is drawn away by his own desires and enticed. Then, when desire has conceived, it gives birth to sin; and sin, when it is full-grown, brings forth death. Do not be deceived, my beloved brethren.
>
> (James 1:13–16)

3. The Holy Spirit is the "Agent of Change."

These days men pay good money to be told that they are hopelessly victimized by their past or their DNA, but the early Christians freely dispensed the hope found in the Gospel and were confident of the life-changing power of the Holy Spirit. As we take our eyes off ourselves and put them on Christ we are changed into His image by the Spirit of God. "But we all, with unveiled face, beholding as in a mirror the glory of the Lord, are being transformed into the same image from glory to glory, just as by the Spirit of the Lord" (2 Corinthians 3:18).

These core beliefs naturally led the early Christians to practice what is referred to as *nouthetic counseling*. The nouthetic approach to counseling grows out of two NT words: *noutheses* and *noutheteo*. The words mean "to warn, to admonish, or to exhort." They imply an aspect of *confrontation* so as to effect change. Jay Adams asserts that this approach to helping people contains three basic elements.[16] First, it presupposes a need for change, that there is something in the life that God wants changed. Second, problems are solved by verbal means; that is, the stress is placed on "what"—"What is wrong?" And, "What needs to be done about it?" The Word spoken in encouragement, admonishment, or rebuke renews the mind, which leads to transformation of life. Third, the purpose for counseling is always that the counselee benefits by seeking to change that in his life which hurts him. When this kind of ministry is examined in the New Testament, three principles become obvious.

a. **Pastors are required to counsel and equip others to be counselors.**
   Pastoral ministry involves constant admonition. No matter how hard we may try, pastors cannot get out of counseling people. The Ephesian elders were told

to remember: "that for three years I did not cease to warn everyone night and day with tears" (Acts 20:31). Those were not tears of joy, but grief, anguish, and concern. Paul's corrective letters to the Corinthians were motivated by his love and concern for them (1 Corinthians 4:14). He accepted confrontation and teaching as steps in the process of presenting people to God as "complete" in Christ (Colossians 1:28 NASB) and referred to this kind of ministry as intense "labor" (1 Thessalonians 5:12). The pastor's responsibility to equip the saints for the work of ministry (Ephesians 4:12) also includes the task of training fellow believers to counsel biblically.

b. **Every believer is expected to be a counselor.**
The ministry of counseling is not only for pastors. In fact, every believer is expected to be involved in it to some degree. The Apostle Paul was confident that well-taught believers are "able to counsel one another" (Romans 15:14 NASB). A growing Christian with a love for, and a working knowledge of, Scripture is a far more competent counselor than a trained psychologist with three degrees hanging on his wall and several initials behind his name, whose confidence is in man-centered theories and practices. Effective counseling is the product of being richly indwelt by the Word of God (Colossians 3:16), not the theories of Sigmund Freud or Carl Jung. Far from giving pat answers like, "Take two Bible verses and call me in the morning," biblical counseling requires wisdom and compassion from God because real people have real needs (1 Thessalonians 5:14).

63

c. **The local church is the intended and ideal place for counseling.**
God has also provided the ideal environment where lives may be changed. It is not an accident that the commands to counsel one another are found in letters to local churches. The apostles assumed every believer would be a faithful member of a local body of Christ and the New Testament never even entertains the idea of a Christian not being accountable to a group of fellow believers. The book of Hebrews, written to a local body of Jewish believers, stresses the immense value of this relationship, "and let us consider one another in order to stir up love and good works, not forsaking the assembling of ourselves together, as is the manner of some, but exhorting one another" (Hebrews 10:24, 25).

The local church is the ideal place for developing a counseling ministry. It is also the ideal place for you to be trained to counsel others. If you are not already, get involved with a vibrant, Bible teaching church where you can mature in Christ and be equipped to serve others.

CHAPTER TWELVE

Why God Creates Hearing-Impaired Children

Meditation on my infant daughter and
the bedrock truth of Exodus 4:11

"So the LORD said to him, 'Who has made man's mouth?

Or who makes the mute, the deaf, the seeing, or the blind?
Have not I, the LORD?'"
—*Exodus 4:11*

Two months ago, when our baby's hearing impairment was confirmed, I immediately began thinking about the sovereignty of God in creating the deaf. My thoughts quickly turned in remembrance to the above words, spoken by God to Moses. If God takes credit for making some people deaf, I concluded, He must have very good reasons for it and, therefore, it is not our place to question His holy purpose, but instead to glory in His infinite wisdom. Trusting God in the journey of life means holding on tightly to simple bedrock truths we can count on no matter what may change in our circumstances. Exodus 4:11 is, for us, one of those bedrocks.

Last month the degree of our daughter's impairment was determined to be profound, the classification closest to total deafness. We are grateful there is at least a little hearing ability, which we are told should be able to be activated by aids, though it is uncertain how much they will help and how her speech development will be affected. We are thanking the Lord, not only for His perfect wisdom in all of creation, but also for being so gracious to mankind that such a wealth of knowledge about the human ear, as well as innovative ways to assist the hearing-impaired, now exist.

Our response is not stoic, indifferent to emotion, neither are we guilty of what some label "denial." Our emotions are real. When we realize that of the hundreds of times we have told her we love her, she has not heard us once, there is a pain felt deep inside that words fail to describe. But God knows how much we treasure this gift of our daughter, and she knows it, too. As we trust Him, resist the temptation to lean on our own understanding, and consciously acknowledge Him in all our ways, He is always faithful to direct our paths (Proverbs 3:5, 6).

Of course there are questions we cannot answer, but this one thing we do know: our God is the all-wise and good Creator, whose purposes and counsel far exceed ours. When He knit our little Kayte in her mother's womb, it appears He allowed genetic weaknesses to determine her impairment and did so with all her days "fashioned" in mind (Psalm 139:13–16). And, in knowing this, there really is not much more we need to know. It is enough to know God has His reasons; I don't have to try to manufacture them for my own sake. He is God and I am not and the more often I recognize this, the more I will truly walk by faith.

But as I've contemplated God's right to create the hearing-impaired, thoughts have jelled in my mind, generating some reasons He *might* choose to do so for our benefit and His glory. So, in addition to training us to rest in the absolute sovereignty of God, there are at least seven other benefits that dealing with hearing impairment could bring:

1. So that we learn patience and compassion.

Therefore, as the elect of God, holy and beloved, put on tender mercies, kindness, humility, meekness, longsuffering.

(Colossians 3:12)

If there were no deaf people in the world we would lose the opportunity to learn patience and clothe ourselves with compassion. To be more specific, if our oldest son, Kenan, had not been hearing-impaired, I highly doubt that the rest of us in the family would be ever-conscious of making eye contact and speaking clearly to his face, instead of simply shouting at his back. We also would not have learned to repeat ourselves without a sigh or an impatient tone in our voice, and "never mind" would still be in our allowable family vocabulary. I like to think hearing-impairment is helping us become clearer speakers and more considerate listeners and, therefore, that our family is stronger because of it.

2. So we grasp the importance of each member of the body.

For in fact the body is not one member but many. If the foot should say, "Because I am not a hand, I am not of the body," is it therefore not of the body? And if the ear should say, "Because I am not an eye, I am not of the body," is it therefore not of the body? If the whole body were an eye, where would be the hearing? If the whole were hearing, where would be the smelling? But now God has set the members, each one of them, in the body just as He pleased. And if they were all one member, where would the body be? But now indeed there are many members, yet one body.

(1 Corinthians 12:14–20)

Hearing impairment gives us the opportunity to see how important each and every part of the human body is, as it often results in the strengthening of the other senses. We have seen this in Kenan, whose impairment is slightly less severe than our daughter's. His visual memory far exceeds that of the rest of us and his engagement in verbal conversation is much more deliberate as he *sees* words in addition to hearing them by reading the lips of those who speak. And he takes far less for granted. It is clear his other senses are compensating for the weakness of the ear. Even though Kayte is only five months old, we have already noticed that visual stimulation is very important to her (she likes to be able to see us), as is touch (she takes comfort in knowing we are there because she cannot hear our voices in the room). All this serves as a vivid reminder of God's design of the local church as an interdependent body: many parts working together, showing preference to one another in honor, that the whole body might bring more glory to God. Perhaps hearing-impairment is meant to teach all of us "to bear the weaknesses of those without strength and not *just* please ourselves" (Romans 15:1 NASB).

3. **To appreciate God's value of human life and rework our definition of "normal."**

> Then God said, "Let Us make man in Our image."
>
> (Genesis 1:26)

> For the Lord does not see as man sees; for man looks at the outward appearance, but the LORD looks at the heart.
>
> (1 Samuel 16:7)

It is no secret that our society places a huge emphasis on being "normal," whatever *that* is, and that we tend to measure the value of others by whether or not they are physically appealing or "free from defect." But what if God looks at things differently? What if all human life is equally valuable—simply because it is created in His image? What if He does not place all that much value on body parts functioning *normally* because He is instead looking at the heart? And what if physical disabilities are of no matter to God in the first place? Perhaps hearing-impairment challenges us to adjust our value of human life by the *image-of-God-stamp* it bears and to place a higher priority on the inner person. If so, it is a blessing to us.

4. **To confound the worldly-wise and display His power and glory.**

> Now as Jesus passed by, He saw a man who was blind from birth. And His disciples asked Him, saying, "Rabbi, who sinned, this man or his parents, that he was born blind?" Jesus answered, "Neither this man nor his parents sinned, but that the works of God should be revealed in him."
>
> (John 9:1–3)

It can get no clearer than this. God chooses to do what He does for His own glory. As He created this man blind from birth, so He creates the deaf in order that His works might be displayed through them. God displays His power against the backdrop of human weakness in order to reveal that it is brighter and more worthy of honor and praise. Long before He took credit for creating the deaf, Moses argued with Him, "O my Lord, I am not eloquent, neither before nor since You have spoken to Your servant; but I am slow of speech and slow of tongue" (Exodus 4:10). Moses thought God's choice of himself as a public speaker was a poor one until he came to grips with just who *he* was and who *God* is. God is God, and Moses was not. God creates people for His purposes and, if we are willing, uses us, *with* all our impairments, to confound the world's wisdom. The world may think disabled people are less important, but our God knows better. "Therefore most gladly I will rather boast in my infirmities, that the power of Christ may rest upon me," Paul said. (2 Corinthians 12:9).

5. **To remind us to look forward to Jesus' Second Coming and our own resurrection.**

    So also is the resurrection of the dead. The body is sown in corruption, it is raised in incorruption.... So when this corruptible has put on incorruption, and this mortal has put on immortality, then shall be brought to pass the saying that is written: "Death is swallowed up in victory."
    (1 Corinthians 15:42, 54)

Hearing impairment in our family serves as a constant reminder of the temporal nature of our bodies. These bodies, presently living under the curse of Adam, will one day be resurrected by the "Second Adam," Jesus Christ, to be glorified in His Presence when He returns. Scripture assures us: "Beloved, now we are children of God; and it has not yet been revealed what we shall be, but we know that when He is revealed, we shall be like Him, for we shall see Him as He is" (1 John 3:2). For many years Kenan has anticipated the angels' singing as the very first thing he will hear with crystal clarity.

6. **To teach us humility and to encourage others.**

    And lest I should be exalted above measure by the abundance of the revelations, a thorn in the flesh was given to

70

me, a messenger of Satan to buffet me, lest I be exalted above measure.

(2 Corinthians 12:7)

The Apostle Paul accepted his *thorn in the flesh* as a gift from God because it kept him from exalting himself. In other words, it kept him humble. One of the hidden blessings of hearing-impairment may very well be its promotion of an ever-present dependence on God, thus fighting the natural growth of our pride.

For example, there is often a parental pride that flairs up when at first you realize your child may be judged by the world as inferior or teased by other children, whose eyes naturally zero in on differences. This parental pride must be vigilantly opposed and any feelings of self-pity immediately judged as self-serving and, therefore, to be forsaken. Or consider the many hearing-impaired adults too proud to admit they need, or too vain to wear, hearing aids. Why should this be? As stubbornness breeds frustration in the lives of those around them, we thank God for hearing aids and can't imagine family life without them.

If my wife or I ever get to the point of needing them, I trust it will be a natural transition for us. How odd it would make our impaired children feel if they knew we thought it was OK for them to need aids, but we were too ashamed to wear them ourselves! We hope our hearing-impaired children will free others from the fear of man and encourage them to take advantage of the God-given knowledge of modern medical science.

7. **To help us rejoice with those who rejoice.**

Rejoice with those who rejoice, and weep with those who weep.

(Romans 12:15)

71

Biblical compassion is not only empathetic toward those who struggle, but also others-focused enough to rejoice when God does good things for them. Allow me to share one personal example: I hope time never erases the memory of stopping at a toy store on the way home from getting Kenan's first pair of hearing aids. As we walked into the metal-roofed store the gentle sound of rain escaped us, but it was completely new to him and he frequently looked upward in wonder. My wife will never forget what happened a few days later when she saw her toddler walking around the kitchen, touching each cabinet, the dishwasher and stove, and then finally his face—glowing with satisfaction when he found the source of the hum he had never heard before—a vibrating refrigerator!

Witnessing Kayte's world open before her has been less dramatic because of her age, but equally joy-producing for all of us as her sense of awareness immediately increased. She was a fussy baby at first from all the fiddling with her ears, and she also scared herself with her own cry, which resulted in her screaming. Once calmed down, she seemed more alert and observant. Now, instead of her eyes just wandering back and forth, she is making eye contact with us as we speak to her, connecting the sound with the movement of our mouths, prompting more frequent smiles.

Kayte is also more vocal; perhaps she is just fascinated with her own voice and can't believe such sounds are coming from herself. We all agree she is surprised that her family is so loud! I am frequently asked if she is turning to the sound of her name, to which I reply, "She does not know her name yet. She has never heard it before." I don't think this fact had even dawned on us until now, spurring us on to rejoice with her even more.

I want to thank all who have rejoiced with us on this journey of discovery through our children's experience of hearing impairment. As a family, we continue to value your faithful prayers, support, and encouragement as we travel on together with Kayte. We know the Lord has a special plan for Kenan and Kayte's lives and that He will use each one—in His unique, special way—to glorify His Name.

CHAPTER THIRTEEN

From Womb to Tomb

The constant reality of suffering

I n my Bible reading earlier this year I was struck by a
verse I hadn't noticed before. It read: "I should have been
as though I had not been, carried from womb to tomb"
(Job 10:19 NASB). These are the words of the suffering Job
as he voiced his protests to God. Having lost every earthly
belonging and all ten of his children—and presently being
surrounded by "miserable comforters" (16:2)—he regretted
ever being born. Hear Job's lament:

> "My soul loathes my life; I will give free course to my
> complaint, I will speak in the bitterness of my soul"
> (10:1). "Your hands have made me and fashioned me, an
> intricate unity; yet You would destroy me. Remember, I
> pray, that You have made me like clay. And will You turn
> me into dust again?" (10:8, 9). "You renew Your witnesses
> against me, and increase Your indignation toward me;
> changes and war are ever with me. Why then have You
> brought me out of the womb? Oh, that I had perished
> and no eye had seen me!"
>
> (Job 10:17, 18)

Intense, prolonged suffering can bring believers to the point of despair, filled with protest, and wishing they had been carried directly from the womb to the tomb. This is the constant reality of suffering. The Apostle Peter understood this and counseled his afflicted readers:

> In this you greatly rejoice, though now for a little while, if need be, you have been grieved by various trials, that the genuineness of your faith, being much more precious than gold that perishes, though it is tested by fire, may be found to praise, honor, and glory at the revelation of Jesus Christ, whom having not seen you love. Though now you do not see Him, yet believing, you rejoice with joy inexpressible and full of glory, receiving the end of your faith—the salvation of your souls.
>
> (1 Peter 1:6–9)

This passage teaches us seven truths about trials:

1. **Trials are temporary (". . . *now for a little while*").**

We need to view earthly trials as "light affliction, which is but for a moment... working for us a far more exceeding and eternal weight of glory, while we do not look at the things which are seen, but at the things which are not seen. For the things which are seen are temporary, but the things which are not seen are eternal" (2 Corinthians 4:17, 18). By the pain of suffering, God reminds us of the eternal weight of glory awaiting us and by doing so sends a new dose of lovingkindness and compassion, new mercy every morning. Great is His faithfulness! (Lamentations 3:22, 23).

2. **Trials are necessary** (". . . *if need be*").

God in His infinite wisdom knows exactly what kinds of trials must be designed to stimulate the growth necessary for our own spiritual health. Paul was given a *"thorn in the flesh"* and, though he did not enjoy it, God assured him it was the necessary treatment to stunt the growth of his cancerous pride, lest he become useless to God. Through it all he would learn that God's grace was sufficient (2 Corinthians 12:7–10). Greek scholar Kenneth Wuest wrote, "To those servants of God whom He purposes to use in a larger, greater way, many trials are allowed to come, for 'we must be ground between the millstones of suffering before we can be bread for the multitude.'"[17]

3. **Trials are distressing** (". . . *you have been grieved*").

There is no pretending here. Peter knew his readers were *grieved.* The word does not refer to the suffering itself, but to the mental effects of suffering, which many times are worse. The Psalmist knew and admitted this. "Reproach has broken my heart, and I am full of heaviness; I looked for someone to take pity, but there was none; and for comforters, but I found none" (Psalm 69:20). "My soul clings to the dust . . . my soul melts from heaviness" (Psalm 119:25, 28). Job said, "If I say, 'I will forget my complaint, I will put off my sad face and wear a smile,' I am afraid of all my sufferings; I know that You will not hold me innocent" (9:27, 28). The pain of suffering often compels us to search our hearts to see what may need to be cleansed by God through honest confession.

4. **Trials are diverse** (". . . *various trials*").

Trials come in all shapes and sizes. Sometimes they afflict our bodies and other times our minds. Sometimes they disturb our comfort zones and other times our loved ones. Trials may come from God. Job said to his grieving wife, "Shall we indeed accept good from God, and shall we not accept adversity?" (2:10). Trials may come from Satan (as permitted by God). Paul's "thorn in the flesh" came via, "a messenger of Satan" sent to "buffet" him (2 Corinthians 12:7). Trials may come from the world: Jesus warned, "If you were of the world, the world would love its own. Yet because you are not of the world, but I chose you out of the world, therefore the world hates you" (John 15:19). Trials may also come from our own disobedience. "For whom the LORD loves He chastens, and scourges every son whom He receives. . . . Now no chastening seems to be joyful for the present, but painful; nevertheless, afterward it yields the peaceable fruit of righteousness to those who have been trained by it" (Hebrews 12:6, 11).

5. **Trials are refining** (". . . *though it is tested by fire*").

God's purpose in suffering is "that the genuineness of [our] faith, being much more precious than gold that perishes, though it is tested by fire, may be found to praise, honor, and glory at the revelation of Jesus Christ." God does not ordain trials to set us up for failure but to prove the reality of our faith in a way similar to the process of purifying metals, our faith being more precious than gold itself, which is perishable. Kenneth Wuest provides a great illustration:

77

The picture here is of an ancient goldsmith who puts his crude gold ore in a crucible, subjects it to intense heat, and thus liquefies the mass. The impurities rise to the surface and are skimmed off. When the metalworker is able to see the reflection of his face clearly mirrored in the surface of the liquid, he takes it off the fire, for he knows that the contents are pure gold. So it is with God and His child. He puts us in the crucible of Christian suffering, in which process sin is gradually put out of our lives, our faith is purified from the slag of unbelief that somehow mingles with it so often, and the result is the reflection of the face of Jesus Christ in the character of the Christian. This, above all, God the Father desires to see. Christlikeness is God's ideal for His child. Christian suffering is one of the most potent means to that end.[18]

When we submit to the will of God in our trials, we learn to say with Job, "When He has tested me, I shall come forth as gold" (Job 23:10).

6. **Trials are faith-building** (". . . *whom having not seen you love*").

Christians can rejoice in the midst of trials because even though we do not see God we believe in Him. This faith produces joy that exceeds speech and is full of glory—even in the face of pain. "And not only that, but we also glory in tribulations, knowing that tribulation produces perseverance; and perseverance, character; and character, hope. Now hope does not disappoint, because the love of God has been poured out in our hearts by the Holy Spirit who was given to us" (Romans 5:3–5).

7. **Trials are beneficial** (*receiving the end of your faith—the salvation of your souls*)

Suffering proves the genuineness of faith, which ultimately results in salvation. Trials not only prepare us for eternity, but they make us ache for it.

> For I consider that the sufferings of this present time are not worthy to be compared with the glory which shall be revealed in us. For the earnest expectation of the creation eagerly waits for the revealing of the sons of God. . . . For we know that the whole creation groans and labors with birth pangs together until now. Not only that, but we also who have the first fruits of the Spirit, even we ourselves groan within ourselves, eagerly waiting for the adoption, the redemption of our body.
>
> (Romans:18, 19; 22, 23)

In the end Job learned a priceless lesson. How different his words to God sound now: "'I have heard of You by the hearing of the ear, but now my eye sees You. Therefore I abhor myself, and repent in dust and ashes'" (Job 42:5, 6). Job no longer wishes he were dead because he now has 20/20 faith. He sees his trial as a gift from above sent for *his* good and God's glory. Do you?

CHAPTER FOURTEEN

The Unsearchable Ways of God

A poem birthed by tragedy

The following poem was written in memory of Rachel Matt, one of the ten who lost their lives on October 11, 2002, in the worst automobile accident in Wisconsin history. Rachel's family encouraged me to share it with the rest of you since God has been so gracious to use it to strengthen their faith.

> *Sometimes God's ways are hard to understand,*
> *We want to ask "Why?"—to follow His hand.*
> *Sometimes when tragedy comes from above,*
> *It tempts us to waver, to doubt His love.*
>
> *But God is infinitely wise and good,*
> *He is too lofty to be understood.*
> *His love is endless. His kindness is great.*
> *He is too wise to leave one thing to fate.*
>
> *Though His purpose may be unknown to us,*
> *We cling to the Rock; in Him we must trust.*

To Him we can run; with Him we can plead,
An ever-present help in time of need.

Our hearts they ache; our minds they probe,
But ultimately we must learn from Job:
The Lord Who gives can also take away,
His Name is to be blessed each and every day.

We may wonder why He would make us weep,
His ways are unsearchable; His knowledge deep.
So freely cry! Tears and grief are His gifts,
By His grace He heals; by His strength He lifts.

—*October 14, 2002*

[Based on Romans 11:33; Psalm 46:1, 18:2; Job 1:21]

CHAPTER FIFTEEN

Sex, Lust, and the Slaughterhouse

Can a man play with fire and not get burned?

A man may be a rising superstar in the world of sports or a powerful corporate CEO until his sin surely finds him out and, by admission of adultery, he begins to be "reduced to a crust of bread" (Proverbs 6:26). As reward for his unfaithfulness, God's Word promises only self-destruction and lasting disgrace to the adulterer. The Scripture is clear on this matter, asking:

> Can a man take fire to his bosom and his clothes not be burned? Can one walk on hot coals, and his feet not be seared? So is he who goes in to his neighbor's wife; whoever touches her shall not be innocent. People do not despise a thief if he steals to satisfy himself when he is starving. Yet when he is found, he must restore sevenfold; he may have to give up all the substance of his house. Whoever commits adultery with a woman lacks understanding; he who does so destroys his own soul. Wounds and dishonor he will get, and his reproach will not be wiped away.
>
> (Proverbs 6:27–33)

For the lips of an immoral woman drip honey, and her mouth is smoother than oil; but in the end she is bitter as wormwood, sharp as a two-edged sword. Her feet go down to death, her steps lay hold of hell.

(Proverbs 5:3–5)

Remove your way far from her, and do not go near the door of her house, lest you give your honor to others, and your years to the cruel one; lest aliens be filled with your wealth, and your labors go to the house of a foreigner; and you mourn at last, when your flesh and your body are consumed, and say: "How I have hated instruction, and my heart despised correction! I have not obeyed the voice of my teachers, nor inclined my ear to those who instructed me! I was on the verge of total ruin, in the midst of the assembly and congregation."

(Proverbs 5:8–14)

Immediately he went after her, as an ox goes to the slaughter, or as a fool to the correction of the stocks, till an arrow struck his liver. As a bird hastens to the snare, he did not know it would cost his life.

(Proverbs 7:22, 23)

Proverbs says the adulterer lacks understanding and thus destroys himself. When he is finally found out by others, he himself has only found wounds and disgrace. Even if the world opines that it was *just* an affair, his reproach will not be wiped away.

What is the cause of adultery? Lust, pure and simple. Selfish, self-centered, self-gratifying, self-worshiping lust. Bryan Clark, in his exceptional book, *All It's Meant to Be,* writes: "Lustful passion is what causes a person to throw away a marriage for some fling that can't last. It explains why a person will risk disease and even death for a meaningless romp between the sheets. . . . Lust is a cruel

83

taskmaster."[19] *Beware!* The price charged by the taskmaster of lust is heavy indeed.

King David's experience with Bathsheba is a biblical illustration of this fact. In a moment of unguarded lust he committed adultery with her and then killed her husband in an attempt to cover up his sin. God then sent Nathan, the prophet and counselor, to confront David, and he repented and received the cleansing power of God's forgiveness. The prophet said, "*The LORD also has put away your sin,* but he also said the child *who is born to you shall surely die*" (2 Samuel 12:13, 14). The death of his infant son was only the beginning of the consequences David suffered. He would never live another day without the presence of violence within his family.

All of this should serve as a very sober reminder to us of the subtle and deceitful power of sin. Sin always promises great and wonderful pleasures, but never tells us they will last only for a moment and then be followed by long-term pain and suffering beyond imagination. Our hearts are "deceitful above all things" (Jeremiah 17:9). They, along with the devil, too often convince us that a little lust is all right. However, lust is never content to exist in small quantities. Its sole desire is to master our hearts so completely that unlawful actions work themselves out as if they are perfectly natural.

Therefore, we must consistently renew our minds with God's truth. "How can a young man keep his way pure? By keeping it according to Your word" (Psalm 119:9 NASB). Also:

- We must keep talking to ourselves about how God is so jealous for the purity of the marriage bed that Old Testament law required the death penalty for adulterers and adulteresses (Leviticus 20:10), and the New Testament promises, "God will judge" (Hebrews 13:4). "For why should you, my son, be enraptured by an immoral woman, and be embraced in the arms of a seductress? For the ways of man are before the eyes of the LORD, and He ponders all his paths. His own iniquities entrap the wicked man, and he is caught in the cords of his sin. He shall die for lack of instruction, and in the greatness of his folly he shall go astray" (Proverbs 5:20–23).

• We must continually watch over our hearts with all diligence, "for out of it spring the issues of life" (Proverbs 4:23). The only way to do this is to guard what comes into the mind. Kent Hughes calls this, "the discipline of refusal."[20] Jesus taught that this is where the battle lies: "You have heard that it was said to those of old, 'You shall not commit adultery.' But I say to you that whoever looks at a woman to lust for her has already committed adultery with her in his heart" (Matthew 5:27, 28).

• We must remind ourselves that God originally designed sex to be the fullest expression of marital love and loyalty. Anything outside of that is less than God's best. "Then the rib which the LORD God had taken from man He made into a woman, and He brought her to the man. And Adam said: 'This is now bone of my bones and flesh of my flesh; she shall be called Woman, because she was taken out of Man.' Therefore a man shall leave his father and mother and be joined to his wife, and they shall become one flesh. And they were both naked, the man and his wife, and were not ashamed" (Genesis 2:22–25).

- We must confess and repent of impure thoughts and actions that easily become seeds which may one day bear rotten fruit. "Wash me thoroughly from my iniquity, and cleanse me from my sin. For I acknowledge my transgressions and my sin is always before me" (Psalm 51:2, 3). Thomas Watson wrote: "Our sorrow for sin must be such as makes us willing to let go of those sins which brought in the greatest income of profit or delight."[21]

- Married couples must nurture their relationship and thus build a strong fortress that will not easily be penetrated by the enemy. "Let your fountain be blessed, and rejoice with the wife of your youth. As a loving deer and a graceful doe, let her breasts satisfy you at all times; and always be enraptured with her love" (Proverbs 5:18, 19). "Do not deprive one another, except with consent for a time, that you may give yourselves to fasting and prayer; and come together again so that Satan does not tempt you because of your lack of self control" (1 Corinthians 7:5).

- Singles must resist temptation and stand firm against the devil and his attempts to convince them that sexual pleasure is a greater pursuit than God Himself. "Flee also youthful lusts; but pursue righteousness, faith, love, peace with those who call on the Lord out of a pure heart" (2 Timothy 2:22). "Be sober, be vigilant; because your adversary the devil walks about like a roaring lion, seeking whom he may devour. Resist him, steadfast in the faith, knowing that the same sufferings are experienced by your brotherhood in the world" (1 Peter 5:8, 9).

Let us all beware! Let none of us dare to think we are above succumbing to the incredible power of lust. "Therefore let him who thinks he stands take heed lest he fall" (1 Corinthians 10:12).

CHAPTER SIXTEEN

"The Vomit of the Soul"

The importance of repentance
and confession

In order for lasting change to take place in our hearts there must be what the Bible calls *repentance*. Repentance is the flipside of faith; they go together—two sides of the same coin, "inseparable graces,"[22] two concepts that must not be divorced. In other words, the saving faith of the Bible is a *repentant* faith. There is no turning to God without there also being a turning away from sin.

Repentance is essentially a change of mind but, like faith, it involves the heart of man in its entirety: intellect, emotion, and will. It comes from the Greek word *metanoia, meta* meaning "after," or "change" and *noeo* "to perceive." Literally, it means, "to change one's mind or purpose... always, in the New Testament, involving a change for the better. The subject chiefly has reference to 'repentance' from sin."[23]

The doctrine of repentance is being given a *bad rap* by some people today because it is often confused with *penance*. Penance, paying for one's sin by works of self-punishment, is clearly anti-biblical (Ephesians 2:8, 9; Romans 4:4, 5;

Titus 3:5). However, biblical repentance is not a work of man, but a gift from a merciful God (Acts 5:31, 11:18; Romans 2:4). According to the teaching of Paul, pastor/elders need to be able to gently correct those in errant doctrine so that "God perhaps *will grant them repentance,* so that they may know the truth" (2 Timothy 2:25). Repentance is not a human work but the gracious work of the Holy Spirit preparing sinners to approach a holy God on *His* terms, rather than their own. Neglecting repentance downplays sin, which in turn cheapens the Cross.

Wayne Grudem defines repentance as "a heartfelt sorrow for sin, a renouncing of it, and a sincere commitment to forsake it and walk in obedience to Christ."[24] It is critical that we not view repentance and confession as merely one-time events in the life of a Christian, but rather a constant necessity and a repetitive work of the Holy Spirit, bringing us to an ever-deepening awareness of the depth of our depravity and desperate need of a Savior. The Christian life is no less than an ongoing walk of repentance and confession. As the Spirit convicts us of sin, we in turn confess it to God (i.e., agree that His view of it is correct) and receive His gracious cleansing based on the sacrificial death of Christ. As we meditate on the love Christ showed for us at Calvary, we are compelled to walk in greater obedience to His Word. "For the love of Christ compels us, because we judge thus: that if One died for all, then all died; and He died for all, that those who live should live no longer for themselves, but for Him who died for them and rose again" (2 Corinthians 5:14, 15).

One of the most probing works on repentance I have ever read is *The Doctrine of Repentance* by the English Puritan, Thomas Watson.[25] This seventeenth century pastor used vivid word pictures to penetrate my soul and bring me to a deeper understanding of my heart. Let me pass along some of his thoughts on repentance and confession, but a word of warning is in order. *Beware!* You may never look at your sin the same way again.

> Repentance is never out of season; it is of as frequent use as the artificer's tool or the soldier's weapon.
>
> (ibid., p. 7)

> Origen [an early church father] calls confession the vomit of the soul whereby the conscience is eased of that burden which did lie upon it. (p. 32)

> A true penitent is a sin-loather. If a man loathe that which makes his stomach sick, much more will he loathe that which makes his conscience sick. It is more to loathe sin than to leave it. One may leave sin for fear, as in a storm the plate and jewels are cast overboard, but the nauseating and loathing of sin argues a detestation of it. Christ is never loved till sin be loathed. Heaven is never longed for till sin be loathed. (p. 45)

> Confession gives vent to a troubled heart. When guilt lies boiling in the conscience, confession gives ease. It is like the lancing of an abscess which gives ease to the patient. (p. 35)

> A piece of lead, while it is in the lump, can be put to no use, but melt it, and you may then cast it into any mould, and it is made useful. So a heart that is hardened into a lump of sin is good for nothing, but when it is dissolved by repentance, it is useful. (p. 76)

> The eye of faith looks on mercy and that thaws the heart. Faith carries us to Christ's blood, and that blood mollifies [soothes the temper]. Faith persuades of the love of God, and that love sets us a-weeping. (p. 122)

May the Holy Spirit so awaken us to the deception of our sin that we are set a-weeping and earnestly desire to turn from its passing pleasure! However, let us never run from sin simply for the sake of running but sprint back to the Cross, where we find love and mercy and grace and cleansing and restored hope. That is what biblical repentance will do for us.

Nothing between my soul and the Savior,
Naught of this world's delusive dream:
I have renounced all sinful pleasure—Jesus is mine!
There's nothing between.

Nothing between my soul and the Savior,
So that His blessed face may be seen;
Nothing preventing the least of His favor:
Keep the way clear! Let nothing between.

Nothing between, like worldly pleasure:
Habits of life, tho harmless they seem,
Must not my heart from Him ever sever—He is my all!
There's nothing between.

Nothing between my soul and the Savior,
So that His blessed face may be seen;
Nothing preventing the least of His favor:
Keep the way clear! Let nothing between.[26]

CHAPTER SEVENTEEN

Approaching the Unapproachable God

The power of "since"

"He who is the blessed and only Potentate, the King of kings and Lord of lords, who alone has immortality, dwelling in unapproachable light, whom no man has seen or can see, to whom be honor and everlasting power. Amen."

(1 Timothy 6:15, 16)

"…let us draw near with a true heart in full assurance of faith, having our hearts sprinkled from an evil conscience and our bodies washed with pure water."

(Hebrews 10:22)

Is it inconsistent for the Bible to teach that God dwells in "unapproachable light" while at the same time exhorting us to approach Him? If God dwells in the white-hot light of His holiness, how can sinners like you and I ever hope to take even one baby step toward Him? If God is so pure, so completely undefiled, so sharply separate from sin, how can we *ever* approach Him? Indeed, He is unapproachable.

Yet, the author of Hebrews strongly encourages us to not only approach God, but to do so with confidence. How can this be? Is this not contradictory? It *would* be if it were not for two words: "since" and "since."

> *Since therefore,* brethren, we have confidence to enter the holy place by the blood of Jesus, by a new and living way which He inaugurated for us through the veil, that is, His flesh.
>
> (Hebrews 10:19, 20 NASB)

The first reason why it is possible to approach the unapproachable God is because Jesus paved the way to God for mankind with His Blood. He tiled a "newly slain way" into God's Presence. *How did He do this?* "Through the veil, that is, His flesh." Through suffering and death, Jesus opened the door to God. By enduring the wrath of God for three long hours of darkness (Luke 23:44, 45), He met the righteous demands of our holy God. By offering the veil of His flesh to be torn, He ripped the veil of the temple in two. By paying the death penalty for sin, He threw open the door into God's Presence.

> ...*and since* we have a great priest over the house of God...
>
> (Hebrews 10:21 NASB)

The second reason (which is really not a second, but is directly tied to the first) is because Jesus is greater than all human priests. The author calls Him a "great" priest because He did not bring a foreign sacrifice to God, but instead offered Himself, "once at the end of the ages, He has appeared to put away sin by the sacrifice of Himself" (Hebrews 9:26).

Only absolute purity would do. Only sinless flesh could satisfy God's justice and mediate for sinners. As High Priest, Christ entered the holy place not made with hands to offer one sacrifice, one time, for all people. As a result, God's holiness, righteousness, and wrath were satisfied. Now all who come to Christ by faith approach God with confidence because they do so through His merit alone. Three days later, God sealed and advertised this new access by raising Christ from the dead (Romans 4:25). Therefore, "we have a great High Priest who has passed through the heavens" (Hebrews 4:14) and "always lives to make intercession" for us (Hebrews 7:25).

Therefore, it is not inconsistent for the Bible to compel us to draw near to God provided it is, "in full assurance of faith." Faith in what? Faith in Whom? Faith must have an object or it has no value. The only faith that gives *full* assurance is faith in Jesus, "the author and finisher of our faith, who for the joy that was set before Him endured the cross, despising the shame, and has sat down at the right hand of the throne of God" (Hebrews 12:2). Why did He sit down? Because His atoning work was complete. The road was paved. The door stands open. *Hallelujah!* What a Savior!

O how He loves you and me! O how He loves you and me!
He gave His life; what more could He give?
O how He loves you; O how He loves me;
O how He loves you and me!

Jesus to Calv'ry did go; His love for sinners to show.
What He did there bro't hope from despair.
O how He loves you; O how He loves me;
O how He loves you and me!

Jesus rose up from the grave; to show His power to save.
All who trust Him will rise to new life.
O how He loves you; O how He loves me;
O how He loves you and me![27]

Does God Change His Mind?

Reconciling difficult Scriptures

Some Scriptures seem to say that God changes His mind. Consider, for example:

And *the Lord was sorry* that He had made man on the earth, and He was grieved in His heart.

(Genesis 6:6)

So *the Lord changed His mind* about the harm which He said He would do to His people.

(Exodus 32:14 NASB)

[God said to Samuel], "*I greatly regret that I have set up Saul as king,* for he has turned back from following Me, and has not performed My commandments."

(1 Samuel 15:11)

[The Word of the Lord came to Jeremiah, saying:] "The instant I speak concerning a nation and concerning a kingdom, to pluck up, to pull down, and to destroy it, if that nation against whom I have spoken turns from its evil, *I will relent* of the disaster that I thought to bring upon it. And the instant I speak concerning a nation and concerning a kingdom, to build and to plant it, if it does evil in My sight so that it does not obey My voice, then I will relent concerning the good with which I said I would benefit it. Now therefore, speak to the men of Judah and to the inhabitants of Jerusalem, saying, "Thus says the LORD: 'Behold, I am fashioning a disaster and devising a plan against you. Return now every one from his evil way, and make your ways and your doings good.'"

(Jeremiah 18:7–11)

[The Word of the Lord came to Joel, saying:] "So rend your heart, and not your garments; return to the LORD your God, for He is gracious and merciful, slow to anger, and of great kindness; and *He relents* from doing harm."

(Joel 2:13)

Then God saw their works, that they turned from their evil way; and *God relented* from the disaster that He had said He would bring upon them, and He did not do it.

(Jonah 3:10)

But other scriptures seem to contradict the above:

And also the Glory of Israel will not lie or change His mind; for He is not a man that He should change His mind.

(1 Samuel 15:29 NASB)

For I am the LORD, *I do not change;* therefore you are not consumed, O sons of Jacob.

(Malachi 3:6)

These seemingly conflicting statements often create questions in the mind of Christians. If God is immutable (unchanging) and omniscient (knowing all), how can He change His mind? *Doesn't that possibility cast doubt on the consistency of His nature and the integrity of His character?* How is He to be trusted in the torrents of life if He changes? In answering these questions, two foundational truths must be recognized:

- **The immutability of God applies to His nature, essence, attributes, and preordained purposes.**

    The Bible makes it clear that the character of God does not change (Psalm 102:26, Malachi 3:6, Hebrews 1:12), and that there is "no variation in Him" (James 1:17). His counsel and purposes stand forever (Psalm 33:11, Isaiah 46:10, Hebrews 6:17), and His unconditional promises are sure (1 Kings 8:56, 2 Corinthians 1:20). His lovingkindness, righteousness, and justice will remain for eternity (Psalm 103:17, Isaiah 28:17).

- **The immutability of God does not prevent Him from changing his dealings with changeable men.**

    Though some of God's promises are unconditional— that is, He will fulfill them regardless of man's actions (Genesis 9:8–11, 15:12–21)—many of the blessings and promises of God are directly dependent upon man's obedience or disobedience (see the above verses). However, this in no way makes man sovereign…or God dependent upon *him*. It is simply God allowing man to operate as a responsible moral agent, as he was created to be.

Therefore, the statements that seem to indicate that God changes His mind are expressions of the *conditional nature* of some of His commands or threats of judgment. In other words, His threats of future judgment upon His disobedient people or His promises of blessing upon His obedient people were tests of the heart-intent of man. Under these circumstances, when man changed for the good or the bad, God dealt with him accordingly. Walter Kaiser explains it well:

> Whenever God does not fulfill a promise or execute a threat that he has made, the explanation is obvious: in all these cases, the change has not come in God, but in the individual or nation…. Repentance in God is not, as it is in us, an evidence of indecisiveness. It is, rather, a change in his method of responding to another person based on some change in the other individual.[28]

Change is for man, not God.

CHAPTER NINETEEN

Could My Marriage Save Anyone?

Meditation on Ephesians 5:32

Could anyone get saved by watching my marriage? That is the question I have been asking myself the past year as the Holy Spirit has repeatedly taken my thoughts back to what the Apostle Paul taught the believers in the Church at Ephesus. After spending ten verses laying out the distinctive roles of husbands and wives, Paul wrote this arresting sentence: "This is a great mystery, but I speak concerning Christ and the church" (5:32).

So, I asked the apostle, "What do you mean, Paul? Do you mean to tell me everything you have just said about marriage is for the sake of something greater?" His answer, as revealed in his letter, is simply: "Yes, that *is* what I mean. The mystery of the one-flesh union in marriage is great, but it is not an end in itself. Marriage was created by God as a visible illustration of an infinitely more important relationship—Christ and His Church." In other words, the Church came *before* marriage.

"But," you say, "how can that be? Marriage was instituted in the second chapter of Genesis and the Church was born

100

in the second chapter of the Book of Acts." That is true from a chronological standpoint, but God is not bound by time. He is above it. He created it. Therefore in the mind of God, the Church existed before the sacred institution of marriage. After all, the Lamb was slain from the foundation of the world (Revelation 13:8)!

It is almost as if the three persons of the Godhead were fellowshipping in perfect and holy contentment; reveling in the Father's marvelous plan to bring immeasurable glory to His Son by means of the redemption of man (whom He had not yet created, but knew would rebel), when all of a sudden an idea flickered in the Divine mind.

"We've got it!" They said. "In order to give Our creatures a glimpse of the wonder of this divine/human relationship, We will create an earthly version of our unity and call it *marriage*. And through this the world will see Christ's love for His Church." This is the "mystery" to which Paul was referring.

Therefore, how a husband treats his wife *is* a form of evangelism. *What do I mean?* Too many Christian husbands are guilty of thinking they are great witnesses for Christ, while at the same time they dishonor their wives by how they speak to them and treat them. We may be foolish enough to deceive ourselves into thinking we are serving the Lord by witnessing to others, but if we do so at the expense of, or as a replacement of, love for our wives, then really we are not being true witnesses, but instead, hypocrites. And Satan loves it! He loves to use our pride to trick us into thinking there is more glory in evangelizing unbelievers in the world than there is in wisely leading and taking manly care of our families. So, we can boast all we want about how many people we witnessed to this week, but the question remains: *Would anyone get saved if all they could see was my marriage?* A question like this pierces through

101

false conceptions and surface spirituality and gets to the heart of the matter in *oh,* such a painful way. But there can be no successful heart surgery without pain.

Christian husbands and wives are types of Christ and His Church. By type, I mean a picture, a representation. As a *type* of Christ, the Heavenly Bridegroom, a husband must embrace the truth that the loving and faithful leadership he gives to his wife and family is a powerful evangelistic tool. Through the sacrificial giving of himself for the welfare of his wife, the world witnesses Christ's love for His Church. As a picture of the Church, a wife must embrace the truth that her quiet, godly submission to her husband's headship is also a powerful tool for evangelism. By graciously following her husband's leadership and authority, the world will be drawn to the Lord, to whom they need to subject themselves. So, let's be man enough (and woman enough) to ask the Divine Surgeon to pick up His scalpel and go to work on us. Let evangelism first begin in our own home!

CHAPTER TWENTY

Measuring Success in Terms of Obedience

Avoiding the trap of result-oriented thinking

Success is measured by obedience, not by the results of that obedience. Let me illustrate. Let's say you become aware of a brother in Christ who is living in sin or is on the verge of making an obviously unwise decision. Love for that brother and reverence for God's Word compel you to exhort him to reconsider his actions in light of Scripture. The sober reminder of Galatians 6:1 is fresh in your mind: "Brethren, if a man is overtaken in any trespass, you who are spiritual restore such a one in a spirit of gentleness, considering yourself, lest you also be tempted."

So, you examine your own heart, your own motives, and reflect on your own sinfulness. You pray that the Holy Spirit will guide your every word in a spirit of gentleness. You also ask Him to prepare the heart of your brother to receive your counsel. Then you go.

Sadly, your heartfelt concern is not received as you had hoped. Instead you are met with indifference, limitless rationalization, antagonism, or possibly even wrath.

Accusations fly in your face at breakneck speed and words are spoken you never knew resided in your brother's heart. You leave confused. You thought you were doing God's will. You wonder how it could be that God's Word did not work. Regretfully, you conclude that you have failed and would have been better off remaining silent. Your conclusion is wrong. And let me tell you why…

- **Success is measured by obedience itself.**

    The very fact you obeyed God's Word in putting feet to your brotherly love makes you successful and wise. Jesus said, "He who has My commandments and keeps them, *it is he who loves Me*" (John 14:21). How can you fail by loving Jesus? By doing what was right, you demonstrated a double love: love for God and love for your neighbor. "Therefore whoever hears these sayings of Mine, *and does them,* I will liken him to a wise man who built his house on the rock" (Matthew 7:24).

- **Success is not measured by the results of obedience.**

    Just because your brother failed to respond in a godly manner does not mean you failed. Though God promises blessing to those who obey His Word, He never said the results of obedience would be comfortable or *always* bear the appearance of success. In fact, perceived success may sometimes be the result of disobedience.[29]

    Moses was forced to learn this painful lesson when he struck the rock in anger instead of speaking to it. The perceived result (gushing water) screamed *success.* However, God pronounced a judgment of failure: "Then the LORD spoke to Moses and Aaron, *'Because you did not believe Me, to hallow Me* in the eyes of the children of Israel, therefore you shall not bring this assembly into the land which I have given them'" (Numbers 20:12). Had you ignored your brother's sin you may have preserved a "friendship," but you would also have failed God.

- **Biblical counsel and correction is not always well-received.**

The seasoned counselor approaches confrontation carefully, hoping and praying with all his heart for immediate repentance and restoration, but he is also honest enough to be prepared for rejection. The book of Proverbs alerts us to the fact that pride and willful sin steel the heart against correction, ultimately leading to destruction. "He who is often rebuked, and hardens his neck, will suddenly be destroyed, and that without remedy" (29:1). "Harsh discipline is for him who forsakes the way, *and he who hates correction will die*" (15:10). "Because they hated knowledge and did not choose the fear of the LORD, *they would have none of my counsel and despised my every rebuke.* Therefore they shall eat the fruit of their own way and be filled to the full with their own fancies" (1:29–31). Rejection of reproof is a window to the heart, revealing pride and love for sin, which stem from a lack of the fear of God.

If, to the best of your knowledge, the basis of your confrontation was biblical truth and the violation of God's laws or principles, and you approached your brother in a spirit of love, humility, and gentleness, you are not responsible for his response. To say it another way, if your manner was not offensive it does not matter if your brother found the content of your rebuke to be so.

105

No one who truly loves God enjoys the ministry of confrontation. None of us longs to be rejected. In fact, we are more naturally inclined to seek acceptance. Thus, rejection can be dangerous water to tread in. If coupled with self-pity, rejection can cripple us. If responded to angrily, it can breed vengeful thoughts. If not guarded against, it can produce a calloused heart that resolves to avoid future pain by remaining silent. The Apostle Paul recognized this danger. Therefore, to the same brethren he warned to, "...withdraw from every brother who walks disorderly" (2 Thessalonians 3:6), he also encouraged: "Do not grow weary in doing good" (3:13).

It is often true that *truth hurts.* However, by God's grace, the honest sinner will in time acknowledge that those who loved him the most are those who took the risk of telling him the truth. Let us find peace in knowing simple obedience makes us a success in God's eyes regardless of the immediate, visible outcome.

CHAPTER TWENTY-ONE

Credit Cards, Grand Pianos, and Waiting on the Lord

When God works for those who wait for Him

A few years ago I'd have done it without batting an eye. I'd have signed on the dotted line and agreed to pay monthly installments for the next five years in order to buy a new piano. But this time I didn't. *Why?* Because God has graciously begun to answer my request to teach me to more consistently wait on Him. Now a baby grand sits in our living room—and it was well-worth waiting for.

One verse that has been particularly helpful to me in my continuous process of growth in the ability to wait on God is Isaiah 64:4. It was John Piper that first brought this key verse to my attention. He said:

> God is a tireless worker. Think of God as a worker in your life. Yes, it is amazing. We are prone to think of ourselves as workers in God's life. But the Bible wants us first to be amazed that God is a worker in our lives: "From of old no one has heard or perceived by the ear, no eye has seen a God besides thee, who works for those who wait for him"

107

(Isaiah 64:4 RSV). God is working for us around the clock. He does not take days off, and he does not sleep. In fact, he is so eager to work for us that he goes around looking for more work to do for people who will trust him: "The eyes of the LORD run to and fro throughout the whole earth, to show his might in behalf of those whose heart is whole toward him" (2 Chronicles 16:9, RSV). God loves to show his tireless power and wisdom and goodness by working for people who trust him.[30]

But this waiting and trusting business is not easy for me. I am somewhat impulsive by nature. When I am convinced I must do something, I simply do it. That is a good quality if kept in check by a certain degree of patience, but the bottom line is, I really don't like to wait. But, as I said, the Lord has been teaching me the value of this virtue.

I purchased my first piano after my first year of college because I had begun taking lessons and was enjoying them. Having started music lessons later than most, I didn't want to lose everything during the summer break so I got my first bank loan and, three years later, became the owner of a Kimball console. A year later, the Lord found me—I became a Christian, and my life was redirected toward marriage and moving out of state to enroll in Bible college. As a full-time student and the sole supporter for my new bride, every moment of my life was consumed. Therefore, practicing the piano was, much to my present regret, the first thing to get tossed out the door. However, my wife was able to resume her piano training for a couple more years, until that piano had to be sold to get some much-needed cash after graduation. It was difficult to part with the only thing I had ever bought new, but reality is reality. Bills must be paid and kids must eat.

After we moved back to Wisconsin a few years later, the Lord provided an older piano that served us well for ten years, but was no longer meeting our needs, with five children playing for five hours a day. The instrument itself had seen better days, and pouring more money into repairs no longer seemed like wise stewardship. So, we knew we needed to get serious about replacing it.

We spent a few months looking at used pianos, comparing them to new, and decided we would go all out and buy a new one. Near winter's end our family visited a large music store that was highly recommended to us. There we found the piano we all wanted—a glossy, black, studio upright that listed for a little less than six thousand dollars.

"But," the saleswoman assured us, "Good news! In two weeks we are having our biggest sale of the year, and this piano will be four hundred dollars less." Though it was tempting to *just do it* that very moment, we decided to wait until the closed-door sale to make our commitment.

That is when the Lord began to go to work for us. Several days before the sale we received a phone call about a used baby grand for sale for six hundred dollars. When we inquired, the owner said it was already sold.

"Oh well," we concluded, "for that price it was probably a hunk of junk anyway. I guess the Lord wants us to buy that new one, after all."

We had every intention to go to the "big sale" and take the plunge, but gradually we sensed a yellow light from the Lord. The day before the sale, the saleswoman called and gently urged us not to miss this once-a-year opportunity. Normally I would have given into the pressure. But for some reason the desire to make the decision that very day was no longer there. Instead there was a desire to wait. I didn't really understand it, but I didn't resent it either. Instead, I asked my wife for counsel, and she too felt caution.

"Let's wait until our bathroom remodeling project is done and the plaster dust has settled," we decided. "Why bring a new musical instrument into a dusty house?" We said *no* and felt total peace.

The next day we received a phone call from the owner of the baby grand informing us that the interested party had changed his mind. It was ours if we still wanted it. We said, "Thank you, Lord," and proceeded to ask a piano repairman to look at it with us. For several hundred dollars more he was able to make it as good as new, so to speak.

When it was all said and done, I remembered how years earlier I had, with Spirit-produced contentment, surrendered my dream of ever owning a baby grand piano. How good God has been to fulfill a personal desire while meeting the need of my children and doing "exceedingly abundantly above all that we ask or think" (Ephesians 3:20)!

Now, I don't want you to misunderstand. I don't think buying a new piano on credit is a sin. I have never agreed with those who teach that all debt is sin. The Bible simply does not support that conclusion. However, it does discourage debt and warns against the bondage it creates:

> The rich rules over the poor, and *the borrower is servant* to the lender.
>
> (Proverbs 22:7)

Scripture also warns against "get rich quick" schemes (Proverbs 28:22), which I also include with the "I must have it *now*" attitude so prevalent in our culture (and in our hearts!). In other words, using credit cards is not sinful, but in some cases it is unwise and can easily disguise the need for us to learn to wait on the Lord. He may have something much more wonderful He wants to do for us. And that may be the greatest danger of "easy credit."

110

As for the piano players in our family, we are very glad that our God is patient with us and that he delights to work for us, if only we will trust and wait on Him to do so.

CHAPTER TWENTY-TWO

The Misery of Misers

Rediscovering the delight of giving

"Ebenezer Scrooge" is forever etched in our minds as a synonym for stinginess. He was, as Charles Dickens masterfully described him, "a tight-fisted hand at the grindstone…a squeezing, wrenching, grasping, scraping, clutching, covetous old sinner!"[31] So stingy was Scrooge that he performed the funeral of his friend and business partner, Jacob Marley, "with an undoubted bargain." Not even Christmas, the most giving time of year, could pry his greedy little hands off his wallet.

> A frosty rime was on his head, and on his eyebrows, and his wiry chin. He carried his own low temperature always about him; he iced his office in the dog-days [the hottest days of summer]; and didn't thaw it one degree at Christmas. External heat and cold had little influence on Scrooge. No warmth could warm, nor wintry weather chill him. No wind that blew was bitterer than he, no falling snow was more intent upon its purpose, no pelting rain less open to entreaty. Foul weather didn't know

where to have him. The heaviest rain, and snow, and hail, and sleet, could boast of the advantage over him in only one respect. They often "came down" handsomely [gave generously], and Scrooge never did.

It was not that he was so extravagant toward himself that he had nothing left for others, for he kept only a small fire (kept his thermostat very low) and lit his apartment with a single candle. He turned the lights off and sat in the dark because, "darkness is cheap." No, it was deeper than that.... The Ghost of Christmas Past helped him recall the insightful words of a fair young woman whom Scrooge had once cared for, but who, in Scrooge's heart, had been displaced by another idol—the "golden one"—being driven in his heart to worship, "the master passion, Gain." As a result Scrooge was the most miserable man in his village.

God's Word reveals the heart condition behind stinginess and warns us that we will experience the same grief Scrooge did if we allow miserliness to creep into our hearts. Let's look at the heart condition behind stinginess. It usually involves:

- **Lack of love for God**

  This people I have formed for Myself; they shall declare My praise. But you have not called upon Me, O Jacob; and you have been weary of Me, O Israel. You have not brought Me the sheep for your burnt offerings, nor have you honored Me with your sacrifices. I have not caused you to serve with grain offerings, nor wearied you with incense. You have bought Me no sweet cane with money, nor have you satisfied Me with the fat of your sacrifices; but you have burdened Me with your sins, you have wearied Me with your iniquities.

  (Isaiah 43:21–24)

113

- **Lack of love for others**

  But whoever has this world's goods, and sees his brother
  in need, and shuts up his heart from him, how does the
  love of God abide in him?

  (1 John 3:17)

- **Self-centered spending habits**

  Then Mary took a pound of very costly oil of spikenard,
  anointed the feet of Jesus, and wiped His feet with her
  hair. And the house was filled with the fragrance of the
  oil. Then one of His disciples, Judas Iscariot, Simon's
  son, who would betray Him, said, "Why was this fragrant
  oil not sold for three hundred denarii and given to the
  poor?" This he said, not that he cared for the poor, but
  because he was a thief, and had the money box; and he
  used to take what was put in it.

  (John 12:3–6)

- **Discontentment and greed**

  Therefore put to death your members which are on the
  earth: fornication, uncleanness, passion, evil desire, and
  covetousness, which is idolatry.

  (Colossians 3:5)

- **Worldly priorities**

  Jesus said, "Do not lay up for yourselves treasures on
  earth, where moth and rust destroy and where thieves
  break in and steal; but lay up for yourselves treasures in
  heaven, where neither moth nor rust destroys and where
  thieves do not break in and steal. For where your treasure
  is, there your heart will be also."

  (Matthew 6:19–21)

- **Lack of genuine saving faith**

  What does it profit, my brethren, if someone says he has faith but does not have works? Can faith save him? If a brother or sister is naked and destitute of daily food, and one of you says to them, "Depart in peace, be warmed and filled," but you do not give them the things which are needed for the body, what does it profit? Thus also faith by itself, if it does not have works, is dead.

  (James 2:14–17)

The Bible also speaks about the painful results of stinginess:

- **Spiritual famine**

  But this I say: He who sows sparingly will also reap sparingly, and he who sows bountifully will also reap bountifully.

  (2 Corinthians 9:6)

  Therefore if you have not been faithful in the unrighteous mammon, who will commit to your trust the true riches?

  (Luke 16:11)

- **Poverty**

  There is one who scatters, yet increases more; And there is one who withholds more than is right, but it leads to poverty.

  (Proverbs 11:24)

  Whoever shuts his ears to the cry of the poor will also cry himself and not be heard.

  (Proverbs 21:13)

- **Personal hurt**

  He who loves silver will not be satisfied with silver; nor he who loves abundance, with increase. This also is vanity. When goods increase, they increase who eat them; so what profit have the owners except to see them with their eyes? The sleep of a laboring man is sweet, whether he eats little or much; but the abundance of the rich will not permit him to sleep.

  (Ecclesiastes 5:10–15)

- **Forfeiture of God's blessing**

  Will a man rob God? Yet you have robbed Me! But you say, "In what way have we robbed You?" "In tithes and offerings. You are cursed with a curse, for you have robbed Me, even this whole nation. Bring all the tithes into the storehouse, that there may be food in My house, and try Me now in this," says the LORD of hosts, "If I will not open for you the windows of heaven and pour out for you such blessing that there will not be room enough to receive it."

  (Malachi 3:8–10)

Soon after Scrooge awoke from his three ghostly visits, he was filled with a joy he had never known before. As he hugged his bed curtains and leaped around his room, speaking in a newly brightened voice, he experienced the truth of Jesus' words: "It is more blessed to give than to receive" (Acts 20:35). Like Ebenezer Scrooge, we sometimes need to rediscover the joy of giving. We need to lavish on God and others the fat of our sacrifices. May we guard our hearts from stinginess and our lives from the misery of misers for: "God loves a cheerful giver" (2 Corinthians 9:7).

116

CHAPTER TWENTY-THREE

Four Reasons You Should Vote

Being a heavenly citizen on earth

I am thankful my father and mother set an example of faithful citizenship for me. From my earliest days I can remember Mom and Dad going to the local town hall to vote. Back then I didn't understand what voting was, or why it was so important to them, but now as an adult and father of seven children I do understand and I, too, want to influence government for the present and future generations.

I must confess that for several years after my conversion I took a very careless approach to voting. But now I take my responsibility seriously and am convinced that Christians should view their voting privilege as a stewardship from God for which, like all other stewardships, they will one day give an account. Therefore, let me give you four reasons you should be a faithful voter:

1. **You should vote in order to promote righteousness and curb sin.**

   "Righteousness exalts a nation, but sin is a reproach to any people" (Proverbs 14:34). "By the blessing of the upright the city is exalted, but it is overthrown by the mouth of the wicked" (Proverbs 11:11). "The king establishes the land by justice, but he who receives bribes overthrows it" (Proverbs 29:4). You should not simply be a *party voter*, either. Instead your choices should be based on the issues that matter most to God—truth, righteousness, and life. As far as I'm concerned a candidate who supports the murder of the unborn is not worthy of my vote, regardless of how good his other positions may be. Voting provides an opportunity for believers in Christ to make a difference for righteousness' sake. When wicked politicians reign, the people will groan (Proverbs 29:2), but let the negligent voter remain silent.

2. **You should vote because the end results are in God's sovereign hands.**

   The prophet Daniel boasted of God: "He changes the times and the seasons; He removes kings and raises up kings; He gives wisdom to the wise and knowledge to those who have understanding" (Daniel 2:21). Some Christians fall prey to fatalism by falsely believing that God will raise and lower rulers with or without their vote. Hence, *why bother?* Solomon gave us this truth: "The lot is cast into the lap, but its every decision is from the LORD" (Proverbs 16:33). It is true God does not need us to accomplish His will, but the fact remains: He has not only ordained the end, but the means to that end. Therefore, if God has granted us the privilege of choosing our rulers, and His Word tells us His ways are sovereign, might He not use His people to bring about His will? As citizens of heaven (Philippians 3:20), our confidence is in God, not government. Therefore, don't just vote. Vote *and* pray.

3. **You should vote as a means of honoring God's servants.**

The Bible says, "Let every soul be subject to the governing authorities. For there is no authority except from God, and the authorities that exist are appointed by God . . . For because of this you also pay taxes, for they are God's ministers attending continually to this very thing. Render therefore to all their due: taxes to whom taxes are due, customs to whom customs, fear to whom fear, honor to whom honor" (Romans 13:1, 6, 7).

Our obligation toward governing authorities is clear: "Honor all people. Love the brotherhood. Fear God. Honor the king" (1 Peter 2:17). We must honor the position of elected leaders as public servants of God and show them respect. One simple way to do that is to take time to vote.

4. **You should vote in order to be salt and light in a sin-spoiled and dark world.**

Jesus said: "You are the salt of the earth; but if the salt loses its flavor, how shall it be seasoned? It is then good for nothing but to be thrown out and trampled underfoot by men. You are the light of the world. A city that is set on a hill cannot be hidden. Nor do they light a lamp and put it under a basket, but on a lampstand, and it gives light to all who are in the house" (Matthew 5:13–15).

You should vote because it is an opportunity to influence earth for heaven's sake. Don't throw away this opportunity by hiding your lamp from the voting booth. Vote and pray, for it is one more way to be a heavenly citizen on earth. See you at the polls!

CHAPTER TWENTY-FOUR

I Want to Help You
Kick the Habit

Biblical counsel for smokers

ear Brother or Sister who wants to quit smoking,

I've been thinking about how best I can help you in your personal battle with nicotine addiction. Occasionally someone will ask me to pray for him or her to gain victory over this habit. Whether or not you have ever asked for my help in this matter, please understand: I am not writing this to "come down" on you, but to come alongside you as a brother who cares and wants to help. As I have counseled and encouraged a number of Christians over the years who wanted to "kick the habit," there are many principles that remain in the forefront of my mind. At the risk of being carelessly accused of being a "legalist," I ask you to consider seven principles that I believe will encourage you in the right direction. Let's look at the first four, taken from the context of 1 Corinthians 6:19, 20:

> Or do you not know that your body is the temple of the Holy Spirit who is in you, whom you have from God, and you are not your own? For you were bought at a price; therefore glorify God in your body and in your spirit, which are God's.

These are probably the most quoted verses in all of Scripture concerning any addiction because of the reference to the body as the *temple of the Spirit*. However, some are quick to point out that the immediate and specific context of this teaching is sexual immorality and, therefore, that it cannot apply to smoking. Not so fast!

It is true the problem of immorality is first in the apostle's mind. However, the larger context is broader and, therefore, has application to many areas. Let me explain. Verses 12–14 give general principles concerning the body, including food. It says:

> All things are lawful for me, but all things are not helpful. All things are lawful for me, but I will not be brought under the power of any. Foods for the stomach and the stomach for foods; God will destroy both it and them. Now the body is not for sexual immorality but for the Lord, and the Lord for the body. And God both raised up the Lord and will also raise us up by His power.

Four key principles emerge from this broader context:

1. The Principle of Liberty

This says all things are lawful, but *not all things are helpful*. Smoking may be lawful for the Christian, but is it beneficial? In light of abundant medical evidence concerning its harmful effects, can you honestly say it is profitable to your physical health? How about spiritual health? Does it enhance your spiritual life? If so, *how?* How is it contributing to your growth in discipleship? How is it making you more like Christ?

2. The Principle of Slavery

This declares that all things are lawful, but the believer should not be willingly *mastered* by anything. The addictive ingredients in cigarettes have the power to enslave. If this were not so, the nicotine patch would not be such a popular aid to those trying to quit. Consider these empowering words:

For if we have been united together in the likeness of His death, certainly we also shall be in the likeness of His resurrection, knowing this, that *our old man was crucified with Him,* that the body of sin might be done away with, that *we should no longer be slaves of sin. For he who has died has been freed from sin.*

(Romans 6:5–7)

3. The Principle of Lordship

This says that not only our souls belong to Christ, but our bodies are also *for the Lord.* Christ died to purchase us, and our reasonable response is to offer our bodies as holy sacrifices to God (Romans 12:1, 2). Therefore, His ownership discourages us from doing anything just for the sake of ourselves. "For none of us lives to himself, and no one dies to himself. For if we live, we live to the Lord; and if we die, we die to the Lord. Therefore, whether we live or die, *we are the Lord's*" (Romans 14:7, 8).

123

4. **The Principle of Resurrection**

   This principle says that our bodies occupy a unique place in God's value system. In the future, God *will also raise us up through His power.* A belief in the Resurrection should produce a proper respect for the body since it will one day be raised for the glory of God. This should not lead to body worship but *will* produce concern for its proper care.

   There are yet three additional biblical principles that apply here:

1. **The Principle of Glory**

   This teaches that the believer is to approach even the most mundane daily activities with the goal of bringing glory to God. "Therefore, whether you eat or drink, or whatever you do, do all to the glory of God" (1 Corinthians 10:31). If glorifying God means magnifying Him before others so that their opinion of Him increases, how does smoking do that? How does your smoking make people think more highly of God?

2. **The Principle of Love**

   Love requires that believers be sensitive to how their actions influence others. I'm not advocating enslavement to the opinions of people but encouraging a healthy consideration of how our actions affect those around us. In other words, how does smoking enhance your Christian testimony? If it does not enhance it, perhaps it detracts from it. How might it hinder a younger person who looks up to you with great respect? How does it help the children you influence? Biblical love willingly surrenders that which may hurt others. "Yet *if your brother is grieved because of your food, you are no longer walking in love.* Do not destroy with your food the one for whom Christ died" (Romans 14:15).

3. The Principle of Stewardship

This principle says we are responsible for how we manage God's money. If *the earth is the Lord's and all it contains* (Psalm 24:1 NASB), can a wise steward justify spending the Lord's money on a habit that brings harm to his created body and is a potential hindrance to his influence for the Name of Christ? If you smoke one pack of cigarettes a day, you are probably spending an average of $100/month on your habit. That could feed a family of four in Ukraine for the same length of time. Nonsmokers save money on insurance premiums, as well. How might the freeing up of these funds help your family—or the Lord's work?

Perhaps the counsel of John Paton, missionary to the New Hebrides Islands, will also prove helpful. One of the island cannibals for which Paton earnestly prayed and whom God converted, was named *Youwili.* Shortly after attending his first Communion service, Youwili came to Paton and said, "Missi [missionary], I've given up everything for Jesus, *except one.* I want to know if it is bad, if it will make Jesus angry; for if so, I am willing to give it up. I want to live so as to please Jesus now... Oh, Missi, I have used it so long, and I do like it so well; but if you say that it makes Jesus angry with me, I will smash my pipe now, and never smoke again!" Paton describes the scene:

125

The man's soul was aflame. He was in tremendous earnest, and would have done anything for me. But I was more anxious to instruct his conscience than to dominate it. I therefore replied, in effect, thus, "I rejoice, Youwili, that you are ready to give up anything to please Jesus. He well deserves it, for He gave up His life for you. For my part, you know that I do not smoke; and from my point of view I would think it wrong in me to waste time and money and perhaps health in blowing tobacco smoke into the air. It would do me no good. It could not possibly help me to serve or please Jesus better. I think I am happier and healthier without it. And I am certain that I can use the time and money, spent on this selfish and rather filthy habit, far more for God's glory in many other ways. But I must be true to you, Youwili, and admit that many of God's dear people differ from me in these opinions. They spend time and money, and sometimes injure health, in smoking, besides setting a wasteful example to lads and young men, and do not regard it as sinful. I will not therefore condemn these, our fellow-Christians, by calling smoking a *sin* like drunkenness; but I will say to you that I regard it as a foolish and wasteful indulgence, a bad habit, and that though you may serve and please Jesus with it, you might serve and please Jesus very much better without it."[32]

Let me offer some additional words of balance. Christians often consider smoking as one of "the bad sins" (as if there is such a thing as a "good" sin). However, there are plenty of other habits that are just as bad or worse, but are more "respectable," simply because they are invisible to man's eye or do not give off an odor. Heart-sins like covetousness, lust, and pride are just a few. To think smoking is somehow worse than these is faulty thinking to be sure, but does that give us sufficient reason not to examine it in light of biblical principles? We are commanded to, "test all things" and to "hold fast what is good" (1 Thessalonians 5:21). I don't want to discourage you, but to help and admonish you to look at your habit through the lens of Scripture. Is it part of the *old man* (Ephesians 4:22) that needs to be put off?

Hoping I have encouraged you,
Pastor Paul

CHAPTER TWENTY-FIVE

Chemical Discipline

ADD and the drugging of America's children

Christian educator, Douglas Wilson, writes in his persuasive book, *A Case for Classical Christian Education:*

Suppose for a moment that some prophet had come out of the wilderness in 1958 and predicted that within a generation one-fifth of the children enrolled in our schools would be doped into docility. The prophet would, of course, have been laughed back to his cave. Yet the spiritual nature of our disease is such that when these things do come to pass, precisely because they *have* come to pass, it is impossible to see them. Before they happen, we cannot see them because they have not yet happened. After they happen, we cannot see them because we *let* them happen, and seeing would now require repentance.[33]

THE RISE OF ADD AND THE
DANGERS OF RITALIN

How did this sad state of affairs come to be? How did millions of children so quickly get labeled with "Attention Deficit Disorder" (ADD) or "Attention Deficit/Hyperactivity Disorder" (ADHD) and drugged into compliance? Wilson explains some of the history that has brought us to this pathetic state:

> In the nineteenth century, our nation established a socialistic system of education, telling parents that they did not have to exercise the same degree of responsibility for their children that they used to. Lo and behold, over time parents began to relinquish more and more of their parental duties, assuming "they" out there somewhere would pick up the slack. Children became increasingly unloved, uncared for, and undisciplined. As the resultant lack of self-control became more evident in schoolchildren, people began to look for alternative means of keeping order. One of the means our modern technocratic society discovered was the ability to hit kids on the head with a chemical rock. As a whole, the government school system has said *yes* to drugs, and students by the thousands found themselves on Ritalin, Prozac, Luvox, Paxil, or other related drugs. In many government school systems, such drugs are actively promoted by the administration as a means of keeping order in the classroom.

> Despite decades of official warnings and supporting research confirming the similarities of methylphenidate (Ritalin) and cocaine, tens of millions of children in the United States have been prescribed this psychotropic drug for a widely accepted yet scientifically unproven mental condition: Attention Deficit/Hyperactivity Disorder (ADHD). Now a recently concluded study at the

Brookhaven National Laboratory (BNL) not only confirms the similarities of cocaine and Ritalin, but finds that Ritalin is more potent than cocaine in its effect on the dopamine system, which many doctors believe is one of the areas of the brain most affected by drugs such as Ritalin and cocaine.[34]

In a civil action suit prompted by the suicide of Jennifer Reynolds, psychopharmacologist Peter R. Breggin, M.D., in a sworn affidavit,[35] affirmed that though the manufacturer of Ritalin calls the drug a "mild" stimulant, it "is among the very most powerful stimulants, comparable to amphetamine and methamphetamine, and even cocaine" (p. 3). He goes on: "Ritalin is among the most dangerously addictive and abuse-prone drugs used in medicine" and, "Among pre-teens, Ritalin abuse now equals cocaine as a cause of admissions to emergency rooms" (p. 4). However, the labeling of the drug leads the consumer to believe it will do him good. Dr. Breggin testified further:

> By using the concepts of "attention deficit" and "distractibility" (as well as other similar concepts), the label implies that Ritalin will help children improve their academic and scholastic achievement. In fact, the evidence is contrary to this; Ritalin often impairs higher cognitive abilities. The label should contain a statement that there is no evidence for improvement in academic or scholastic performance, or learning, and that to the contrary, Ritalin may impair higher level learning. Indeed, the label should also mention that there's no evidence for improvement in a child's psychological or social life, and may in fact impair it (ibid., p. 6).

130

Over a decade earlier Dr. Breggin authored a book entitled *Toxic Psychiatry* in which he gave a brief history of the label "Attention Deficit/Hyperactivity Disorder" (ADHD):

> Hyperactivity (HA) is the most frequent justification for drugging children. The difficult-to-control male child is certainly not a new phenomenon, but attempts to give him a medical diagnosis are the product of modern psychology and psychiatry. At first, psychiatrists called hyperactivity a brain disease. When no brain disease could be found, they changed it to "minimal brain disease" (MBD). When no minimal brain disease could be found, the profession transformed the concept into "minimal brain dysfunction." When no minimal brain dysfunction could be demonstrated, the label became attention deficit disorder. Now it's just assumed to be a real disease, regardless of the failure to prove it. Biochemical imbalance is the code word, but there's no more evidence for that than there is for brain disease.[36]

DOES ANYONE REALLY NEED RITALIN?

Most people are shocked to learn there is no scientific proof that such a thing as chemical imbalance exists. However, the average person has swallowed it—hook, line, and sinker. We have been duped into believing drug-dispensing psychoanalysts are treating a medical problem when in reality no such condition has yet to be established. In his book, *Blame It On the Brain,* Ed Welch, writes: "We know that Ritalin affects a number of areas in the brain, but its mode of action is uncertain. One thing, however, is clear: Ritalin *does not* treat any known chemical deficiency in a child's brain. No one needs Ritalin."[37] When one reads over the list of symptoms of this so-called attention disorder, he is forced to ask, "Are any of these symptoms *not* the same as those which result from laziness or lack of self-discipline?"

It seems to me a sensible and fair conclusion is that the vast majority of children stuck with the labels *ADD* or *ADHD* really just lack self-control. They are easily distracted, not because of some so-called chemical imbalance, but because they have a discipline deficiency; they are prone to leave tasks undone, not because of some imaginary brain dysfunction, but because they have not learned to be responsible individuals. The need is not *chemical control,* but disciplining the mind and body God gave them.

I could not agree more wholeheartedly with what Robert Smith, physician and biblical counselor, has written in *The Christian Counselor's Medical Desk Reference:*

> The diagnosis of ADHD, as in most psychiatric problems, is not based on changes in the body, but on behavior. Even though it is vigorously defended as a disease, there is no proof of any physical abnormality in the body. The medications do not correct any known deficiency or physical abnormality. Medication is not a cure. When there is improvement in behavior, which appears to be a direct result of medication, this gives the impression the problem is solved. If the behavior does not improve or gets worse, the dosage is increased. When this fails, a different medication is considered. However, the medication does not deal with the cause of the problem. It does not help the child learn self-control. The underlying thinking and motives of the child are never addressed. It is easier to put a child on a medication than to take the time to nurture and help build character in him.[38]

Tragically, our current epidemic is another example of psychological counseling's denial of the biblical premise that *human behavior is the product of the heart;* that the root of most "mental" problems is not physiological at all, but spiritual; that God's solution is regeneration by the Holy Spirit and renewal of the mind and heart through meditating on and obeying God's Word. That is where "mental health" begins. But these are core truths the psychiatric industry will never affirm. Unfortunately there are millions of reasons—*called dollars*—for it to quickly label people and dispense drugs that will merely feed sinful behavior.

God's Answer to ADD

God's answer for an easily distracted, wandering mind is not chemical discipline but Holy Spirit-produced self-control. By willing submission to the Word of God, bad habits are gradually replaced with godly ones, resulting in a transformed, disciplined life. Ed Welch hits the nail on the head when he writes: "With many children labeled ADD, the arena of the heart is ignored. Yet isn't it possible that some of what we call ADD is sinful self-indulgence and laziness? Is it possible that a prominent cause of the behaviors is a heart that demands its own way?"[39]

Here is a significant place where genuine biblical counseling parts company with the man-centered approaches of psychological and therapeutic counseling. The former believes God specializes in transforming behavior by changing sinful hearts, while the latter swipes hope from people by neatly placing them into little psychological pigeonholes. Robert Smith laments, "The greatest tragedy of this approach is that it communicates that the Bible has no answers for this problem. Apparently the Holy Spirit cannot do what Ritalin allegedly can. Personal responsibility of both parent

133

and child are negated. Biblical doctrines of God, man, sin, and changing behavior are ignored."[40]

David Powlison skillfully articulates how this approach produces people who then view life merely through biological glasses (people are dysfunctional bodies), instead of spiritual glasses (people are God's image-bearers, both body and soul):

> Psychologized people seek to explain and fix life through some interpretation of human life that excludes God, sin, Christ, sanctification, and the rest of truth. But it is time to update our language a bit. Currently, the biopsychologizing of human life is having a huge effect, both in the culture and the church. We minister to an increasing number of *biopsychologized* people who think about themselves, their spouses, or their children as *bodies* run amok.[41]

As a biblical counselor who is clearly *not* a medical doctor, I am careful to never instruct anyone to simply stop taking their prescribed medications without the cooperation of a discerning physician. Not because I think there is a true physical need for the drugs, but because Ritalin and its cousins are seriously addictive and withdrawal is very real. However, over the years, by God's grace, I have had the privilege of witnessing several individuals in our church gradually weaned and totally freed from their medicated states by using God's Word to help them see the root problems in their hearts and by encouraging them to apply that same Word to their lives. This kind of hope a psychiatrist can never give.

A CALL FOR BIBLICAL ADD:
ACTIVE DISCIPLINE DEVELOPMENT

How then can parents prevent their children from being carelessly labeled and medicated? This is a very doable task for those who desire to follow God's Word rather than the prevailing winds of sin-cursed psychology, but it will require patience and persistence over the long haul. Following are four practical guidelines for biblical child discipline:

1. **Teach and enforce boundaries at a very early age.**

   The book of Proverbs stresses the importance of taking advantage of the early years to instill discipline into children. It says:

   Chasten your son *while there is hope.* (19:18)

   Train up a child in the way he should go, and when he is old [assuming the discipline took place when he was young] he will not depart from it. (22:6)

The sooner a child learns there are behavioral boundaries in life, the sooner he will understand the principle of authority and how to be attentive and submissive to it. Children are happiest when they know their boundaries because they can simply be children without having to worry about playing the role of the parent, as well. One thing we have done to aid in this learning process is to use an existing visual boundary (such as a crack in the driveway or sidewalk) to mark the line they cannot cross when playing outside. Violation of this boundary results in discipline. Having established these limits at a young age, we are able to be more at ease, knowing our children are not playing in the street. When teaching boundaries, be sure to:

- Call the child by name (so he cannot say, "I thought you were talking to Joey."). It also shows more respect than, "Hey, kid!"
- Get and keep eye contact throughout your instructions. This teaches attentiveness and respect for the authority figure who is speaking.
- Speak in the form of commands, *not* questions. Some parents say to their three-year old, "Billy, do you think it is time to go to bed?" It's as if they expect him to reply: "In light of my age and tomorrow's agenda, I think it *is* wise for me to go to bed now." Don't be a lazy parent by letting your children make up *your* mind.
- Get a verbal response of understanding, such as, "Yes, sir," or, "Yes, ma'am." This helps the child begin to understand the principle of accountability, which teaches responsibility.

2. **Model obedience to boundaries in your own life.**

God's Word stresses the importance of parental example:

The righteous man *walks in his integrity;* his children *are blessed* after him.

(Proverbs 20:7)

My son, give me your heart, and *let your eyes observe my ways.*

(Proverbs 23:26)

Example is the most powerful tool in child-training. Living a self-controlled, disciplined life yourself will go a long way toward producing responsible, self-controlled children.

3. **Verbally correct and physically discipline.**

   The word "rod" is used seven times in Scripture in reference to physical discipline, otherwise known as *corporal punishment* (10:13, 13:24, 22:15, 23:13, 23:14, 26:3, 29:15). This stresses the importance of using a neutral object for spanking. A parent should refrain from using his hand to discipline his children. A child must have the security of knowing his parent's hand is for expressing affection. I cringe inside when I see a child duck or back away when his father or mother reaches out to touch him. In our home, we use a small, flat piece of wood that we call "the wisdom paddle." Each of our children has one (because each requested one). Written on one side is their name. On the other side is: "Proverbs 13:24." The children find security in knowing that if daddy does not spank them, God will spank daddy. Prior to receiving discipline the child must understand the *reason* for the spanking, and enough pain (not damage) must be inflicted by the *rod* to discourage future disobedience. This is God's method of developing obedience and self-control—necessary character qualities in the life that pleases Him.

4. **Reaffirm your love through affection.**

   Always be sure each discipline session concludes with plenty of affection and, "I love you" assurances. The purpose of all discipline is to restore the close relationship broken by the act(s) of sin. This is why you should never spank a child and send him to his room. Instead, send him to his room and then go and spank him.[42] At the end of every discipline session, your child must be sure of your love. I often ask my children after a spanking, "Why does daddy spank you?" And they always answer, "Because you love me." This will provide your child great security.

CONCLUSION

Though our children's hearts are bound by the foolishness of sin, we have the privilege of being involved in the process of breaking those chains and imparting God's gifts of self-control and wisdom through the sometimes-exhausting process of faithful discipline. By doing so we will train them to see all of life through biblical glasses and protect them from being held captive by the vain philosophies of men—all the while pointing them to Jesus, our Great Physician, our Redeemer, our Savior, our Healer, our Lord, and our Friend.

"They Reach the Shell, not the Kernel"

The pain of persecution and the protective Presence of God

According to Thomas Brooks, a British Congrega-
tionalist preacher who lived from 1608 to 1680,
church history remembers the extent to which the
early followers of Jesus suffered for their faith. He notes:

Peter was crucified with his heels upward—Christ was
crucified with his head upwards, but Peter thought this
was too great an honor for him to be crucified as his Lord,
and therefore he chose to be crucified with his heels upward; and Andrew was crucified by Egeus, king of Edessa;
and James the son of Zebedee was slain by Herod with the
sword (Acts 12:2); and Philip was crucified at Hierapolis
in Asia; and while Bartholomew was preaching the glad
tidings of salvation, multitudes fell upon him and beat
him down with staves, and then crucified him, and after
all this, his skin was flayed off, and he beheaded; Thomas
was slain with a dart [short lance] at Calumina in India;
and Matthew was slain with a spear, say some, others
say he was run through with a sword; and James the son
of Alpheus, who was called the Just, was thrown down

from off a pinnacle of the temple, and yet having some life left in him, he was brained with a fuller's club; Lebbeus was slain by Agbarus, king of Edessa; and Paul was beheaded at Rome under Nero; and Simon the Canaanite was crucified in Egypt, say some, others say that he and Jude were slain in a tumult of the people; and Matthias was stoned to death; and John was banished into Patmos, (Revelation 1:9), and afterwards, as some histories tell us, he was by that cruel tyrant Domitian cast into a tun [large cask] of scalding lead, and yet delivered by a miracle. Thus all these precious servants of God, except John, died violent deaths, and so through sufferings entered into glory; they found in their own experience the truth of what Christ had foretold concerning their sufferings and persecutions.[43]

This record is a painfully accurate fulfillment of Jesus' warnings to His disciples concerning the reality of being hated for being a Christian:

If the world hates you, you know that it hated Me before it hated you. If you were of the world, the world would love its own. Yet because you are not of the world, but I chose you out of the world, therefore the world hates you. Remember the word that I said to you, "A servant is not greater than his master." *If they persecuted Me, they will also persecute you.* If they kept My word, they will keep yours also.

(John 15:18–20)

But when they arrest you and deliver you up, do not worry beforehand, or premeditate what you will speak. But whatever is given you in that hour, speak that; for it is not you who speak, but the Holy Spirit. Now brother will betray brother to death, and a father his child; and children will rise up against parents and cause them to be put to death. And *you will be hated by all for My name's sake*. But he who endures to the end shall be saved.

(Mark 13:11–13)

The bodily pain endured by our faithful forefathers is almost indescribable. Some heroes of the faith, "…were stoned, they were sawn in two, were tempted, were slain with the sword. They wandered about in sheepskins and goatskins, being destitute, afflicted, tormented" (Hebrews 11:37). Such bodily torture is hard for comfortable Christians in America to imagine.

However, there is another, less visible form of suffering for Christ—the internal, emotional agony that accompanies watching how your suffering affects those closest to you. That was the case for John Bunyan, writer of the enduring classic, *Pilgrim's Progress.* His autobiographical testimony of conversion, *Grace Abounding to the Chief of Sinners,* has recently stirred my heart. During his twelve-year imprisonment for preaching the Gospel, he wrote of the internal pain of being separated from his family, especially his blind daughter, Mary:

…I found myself a man encompassed with infirmities. The parting with my wife and poor children has often been to me in this place as pulling the flesh from the bones [take a moment to think about it!], not only because I am somewhat too fond of these great mercies, but also because I would have often brought to my mind the many hardships, miseries, and needs that my poor family were likely to meet with should I be taken from them, especially my poor blind child, who lay nearer to my heart than all the others. Oh, the thoughts of the hardship my poor blind one might undergo would break my heart to pieces. Poor child, what sorrow are you likely to have for your portion in this world! You must be beaten,

141

must beg, suffer hunger, cold, nakedness, and a thousand calamities, though I cannot now endure that the wind should blow upon you. Yet, recalling myself, I thought that I must entrust you all with God, though it goes to the quick to leave you.[44]

What are we to make of all of this? It seems so strange, so distant from our own peaceful form of Christianity. What we *should* make of it is that persecution is to be anticipated by the practicing believer. Suffering for the sake of the Gospel is an honor bestowed on those who love God wholly. Paul warned young Timothy that, "all who desire to live godly in Christ Jesus *will* suffer persecution" (2 Timothy 3:12). The pursuit of holiness will surely evoke fierce winds of persecution, but Brooks counsels us with massive encouragement:

> All the troubles, afflictions, and persecutions that attend holiness can never reach a Christian's soul, they can never diminish a Christian's treasure; they reach the shell, not the kernel; the case, not the jewel; the lumber, not the goods; the outhouse [outbuilding], not the palace; the ribbon in the hat, not the gold in the purse. The most fiery trials and persecutions can never deprive a Christian of the special presence of God, nor of the light of his countenance, nor of the testimony of a good conscience, nor of the joys of the Spirit, nor of the pardon of sin, nor of fellowship with Christ, nor of the exercise of grace, nor of the hopes of glory (Psalm 23:4; 2 Corinthians 1:8, 9, 12); and therefore certainly they can't hurt a Christian; they can't wrong a Christian in his greatest and chiefest concernments.[45]

Praise be to God who has (already) given us the victory through our Lord Jesus Christ!

CHAPTER TWENTY-SEVEN

Don't Check Your Brain at the Door

Why you should always bring your
Bible to church

I did not grow up in a Bible-believing church. So, bringing a Bible along to worship, much less my *own* Bible, was completely foreign to me. But that changed in the spring of 1984 through the ministry of a home Bible study group that was studying the Gospel of John.

As I walked to the second floor apartment where we were meeting, I brought the only Bible I ever owned, and never read—the one I'd been required to purchase for Confirmation Class. After the Holy Spirit opened my spiritual eyes to the truth of the Gospel, which had been hidden from me for nineteen years, I became convinced of the absolute authority and reliability of God's Word. It also birthed in me the firm conviction that no one should be told to believe certain doctrines unless he can be honestly shown from the Bible that they are worthy of his faith.

If a church's doctrine is not taught from the Bible itself, I'd discovered, then that church is calling its people to a faith that is blind. Worse than that, it is calling people to place their faith in the words of men, not the words of God. If churchgoing people would follow the example of the Berean Jews, there would be far fewer blind people being led by blind leaders headed straight for the pit (Matthew 15:14). Here is what set them apart:

> Then the brethren immediately sent Paul and Silas away by night to Berea. When they arrived, they went into the synagogue of the Jews. These were more fair-minded than those in Thessalonica, in that they received the word with all readiness, and searched the Scriptures daily *to find out* whether these things were so. Therefore many of them believed, and also not a few of the Greeks, prominent women as well as men.
>
> (Acts 17:10–12)

These were not "Berean Christians," as many call them. They were unbelieving Jews who *became* Christians after days of comparing the apostles' preaching to the Old Testament Scriptures. In doing so, Luke says, they were, "more fair-minded than those in Thessalonica," since the Jews in that city didn't even welcome the preaching long enough to check it out (see Acts 17:1–9). The Bereans, however, were discerning converts, because they ran the teachings of men through the filter of Scripture to determine their accuracy. Whatever was *screened out* was *thrown out.* Whatever passed the test was worth holding fast to.

What would happen if every churchgoing American brought his or her Bible to church and used it to check out the biblical integrity of the sermon? The result would be *less ignorance* and *more discernment,* less blind faith and more biblical faith. Maybe you think I'm just skeptical because of my past, but I would rather call it *discerning.* Nineteen years of spiritual ignorance taught me at least one thing: don't place blind trust in any man. You should bring your Bible to church because men are fallible and biblical faith is not blind. No preacher on earth is beyond the possibility of doctrinal error. If you leave your Bible at home you are unable to "test the spirits" (1 John 4:1), and, "examine everything carefully," so that you may, "hold fast to that which is good" (1 Thessalonians 5:21 NASB).

Parents, teach your children this habit early on. My wife and I believe that if our children are old enough to walk, they are old enough to carry their own Bible to church. We start with a small New Testament, the one our pastor gave us when the children were born. It is small enough for little hands to carry and inexpensive enough not to cause too much grief if lost. My wife sewed little cloth bags in which each of our children can carry his Bible and Sunday School papers. As the children have grown older, the Bibles have grown bigger and have become more personal and precious to them. What an immense privilege it is for my wife and me to own a copy of God's Word and be able to bring it to church to hear it proclaimed and explained, setting the example for them.

God wants us to renew our minds through Bible-saturation (Romans 12:2). Let's take Him up on His offer of education in righteousness, rather than be content with ignorance. The church that encourages its people to bring their Bibles and teaches them how to use them will please God by producing mature, discerning followers of Christ. See you next Sunday—with your Bible!

CHAPTER TWENTY-EIGHT

If Daniel Had Worked in a Grocery Store

Holding to your convictions graciously

Six weeks ago our oldest son began a new job as a bagger at a local grocery store. While filling out the application, he asked for my help in choosing what hours he would be available to work. Since we do our best to refrain from normal work on the Lord's Day and instead strive to always be present at the three weekly meetings of our church, he made his preferences to the employer clear, which included not being available to work at all on Sundays or on Wednesday evenings. He wasn't more than a week into the job when his requests were ignored.

So, how did he handle this? I will tell you in a minute, but first I want to remind you of the example of Daniel, that prophet who held to his personal convictions in such a bold, yet meek and gracious, manner.

When Daniel was taken to Babylon to be brought into the court of the king he was probably fifteen years old. As one chosen to become a court servant, he was commanded to submit himself to a rigorous training schedule, which included "a daily provision of the king's delicacies and of the wine which he drank" (Daniel 1:5). But Daniel had certain personal convictions. Earlier, he had made a commitment to himself not to eat the king's rich food or to drink wine. So, what did he do? Did he pound his fists on the table and refuse to eat? Or dump the wine on the floor and act offended? He did neither. Instead, he "sought *permission* from the commander of the officials that he might not defile himself" (1:8 NASB). In other words, he went to the authority figure over him, asked to be exempt from the rule, and presented another option.

The commander of the officials granted the exception and gave Daniel and his three friends permission to pursue the alternative plan. Ten days later, Daniel's plan proved successful and he and his friends "entered the king's personal service" (1:19 NASB).

How did Daniel serve as a role model for my sixteen-year-old son? Like Daniel, he approached the assistant manager responsible for scheduling (who was also his second interviewer), explained the problem, made his request, and thought he'd been understood. But the next week, the same thing happened. So, he tried numerous times to speak to him again, only to find him unavailable. So, he spoke with the woman who had been his first interviewer (who also happened to mention during the interview process that his particular schedule requests would not be a problem). However, it happened yet again. So, since my son is a minor and my signature was required to get his work permit in the first place, I was now forced to get involved.

By now, you are thinking: *Don't tell me you are going to say that didn't work either.* Well, yes. The problem persisted until finally the scheduler confessed he had never seen my son's application and, therefore, had no knowledge of his requests. He informed us of his minimum schedule needs, which were too great a commitment to keep, along with a heavy school load and other work responsibilities. There-fore, the only thing left to do was for our son to write a kind letter of resignation, thanking the company for the opportunity to work for them, explaining he could not meet their minimum hourly demand, and wishing them future success.

Unexpectedly, when news of his resignation reached the ears of the store manager, we received a phone call inquir-ing about the situation. The manager said the requested schedule needs were not a problem and encouraged us to reconsider. We thought it over and decided to present an alternative plan: fewer hours' work and only on certain days. Our son wrote out the plan, presented it to the manager, and his request was granted.

Now the reason I took the time to counsel my son through Chapter One of the Book of Daniel was to show him how sufficient the Word of God is to provide answers to our daily dilemmas. And the reason I took the time to share all of this with you is because too many Christians have not yet learned from Daniel. When confronted with differences at their places of employment, they either quickly get of-fended and walk off the job in a huff, or they silently allow their employer's worldly practices to erode the importance of their own convictions. Both responses sacrifice what is best. The first avoids an opportunity to learn a valuable character-building lesson of self-control and the other often becomes a subtle beginning to a life of compromise.

Let me encourage you to follow Daniel's example. When your convictions are overtly or quietly challenged, keep honoring them. But do it with grace and respect toward those in authority over you.

CHAPTER TWENTY-NINE

The Silent American Sin

Biblical thoughts on gluttony

When was the last time you heard a sermon on gluttony? Better yet, when was the last time I preached one? While it is common for pastors to preach against blatant sins like gossip, anger, immorality, lying, homosexuality, stealing, etc., it is quite unusual to hear anything spoken against one of the silent, but most obvious, sins of our generation: gluttony. In recent years books, newspapers, and radio have been making us aware of the rise of obesity in America, especially among children. In his *New York Times* bestseller, *Fast Food Nation: The Dark Side of the All-American Meal,* Eric Schlosser writes:

> By eating like Americans, people all over the world are beginning to look more like Americans, at least in one respect. The United States now has the highest obesity rate of any industrialized nation in the world. More than half of all American adults and about one-quarter of all American children are now obese or overweight. Those proportions have soared during the last few decades, along with the consumption of fast food. The rate of

obesity among American adults is twice as high today as it was in the early 1960s. The rate of obesity among American children is twice as high as it was in the late 1970s. According to James O. Hill, a prominent nutritionist at the University of Colorado, "We've got the fattest, least fit generation of kids ever."...Today about forty-four million American adults are obese. An additional six million are "super-obese"; they weigh about a hundred pounds more than they should. No other nation in history has gotten so fat so fast. . . . Although the current rise in obesity has a number of complex causes, genetics is not one of them. The American gene pool has not changed radically in the past few decades. What has changed is the nation's way of eating and living. In simple terms: when people eat more and move less, they get fat. In the United States, people have become increasingly sedentary—driving to work instead of walking, performing little manual labor, driving to do errands, watching television, playing video games, and using a computer instead of exercising. . . . Little Caesar's [Pizza] slogan, "Big! Big!" now applies not just to the industry's portions, but to its customers. Over the past forty years in the United States, per capita consumption of carbonated soft drinks has more than quadrupled. . . . In 1972, McDonald's added large [size] french fries to its menu; twenty years later, the chain added *super-size fries,* a serving three times larger than what McDonald's offered a generation ago. . . . Obesity is now second only to smoking as a cause of mortality in the United States . . . about 280,000 Americans die every year as a direct result of being overweight. . . . Obesity has been linked to heart disease, colon cancer, stomach cancer, breast cancer, diabetes, arthritis, high blood pressure, infertility, and strokes. . . . Young people who are obese face not only long-term, but also immediate threats to their health. Severely obese American children, ages six to ten, are now dying from heart attacks caused by their weight. . . . It seems wherever America's fast food chains go, waistlines start expanding.[46]

150

Of course, fast food is not totally to blame for obesity and waistlines are not the only thing negatively affected, either. Increasingly nonexistent in America's families (including Christian families) is the regular practice of enjoying healthy meals at home, around the table, *together*. Not much relationship-building interaction can take place while a family is shoveling down greasy fries in the van on the way to the next thing on the schedule. Whatever the causes and effects, no one can deny we are a gluttonous nation.

Webster's New World Dictionary defines gluttony as, "the habit or act of eating too much." Granted, not all obesity is the direct result of gluttony. There are medically organic reasons why some people struggle with weight control more intensely than others. But setting aside that reality, we must still conclude that a great deal of America's health problems are probably caused by the "silent sin" of gluttony. So how does God's Word counsel us?

BIBLICAL OBSERVATIONS CONCERNING GLUTTONY

- **Gluttony is associated with laziness.**

    One of them, a prophet of their own, said, "Cretans are always liars, evil beasts, *lazy gluttons.*"

    (Titus 1:12)

- **Gluttony is one of the addictions associated with the wicked, earthbound, and self-loving.**

    And they shall say to the elders of his city, "This son of ours is stubborn and rebellious; he will not obey our voice; he is a glutton and a drunkard." Then all the men of his city shall stone him to death with stones; so you

151

shall put away the evil from among you, and all Israel shall hear and fear.

(Deuteronomy 21:20, 21)

For many walk, of whom I have told you often, and now tell you even weeping, that they are the enemies of the cross of Christ: whose end is destruction, *whose god is their belly,* and whose glory is in their shame—who *set their mind on earthly things.*

(Philippians 3:18, 19)

Woe to them! For they have gone in the way of Cain, have run greedily in the error of Balaam for profit, and perished in the rebellion of Korah. These are spots in your love feasts, while they feast with you without fear, *serving only themselves.*

(Jude 11, 12)

- **Gluttony abuses God's gifts by succumbing to super-sized consumption.**

Now a wind went out from the LORD, and it brought quail from the sea and left them fluttering near the camp, about a day's journey on this side and about a day's journey on the other side, all around the camp, and about two cubits above the surface of the ground. And the people stayed up all that day, all night, and all the next day, and gathered the quail (he who gathered least gathered ten homers); and they spread them out for themselves all around the camp. But while the meat was still between their teeth, before it was chewed, the wrath of the LORD was aroused against the people, and the LORD struck the people with a very great plague. So he called the name of that place Kibroth Hattaavah, because there they buried the people who had yielded to craving.

(Numbers 11:31, 34; see also Psalm 78:31)

152

- **Gluttony can produce worldly security.**

And in that day the Lord GOD of hosts called for weeping and for mourning, for baldness and for girding with sackcloth. But instead, joy and gladness, slaying oxen and killing sheep, eating meat and drinking wine: "*Let us eat and drink, for tomorrow we die!*" Then it was revealed in my hearing by the LORD of hosts, "Surely for this iniquity there will be no atonement for you, even to your death," says the Lord GOD of hosts.

(Isaiah 22:12–14)

And I will say to my soul, "Soul, you have many goods laid up for many years; *take your ease; eat, drink, and be merry.*" But God said to him, "Fool! This night your soul will be required of you; then whose will those things be which you have provided?"

(Luke 12:19, 20)

But if that servant says in his heart, "My master is delaying his coming," and begins to beat the male and female servants, and to eat and drink and be drunk, the master of that servant will come on a day when he is not looking for him, and at an hour when he is not aware, and will cut him in two and appoint him his portion with the unbelievers."

(Luke 12:45, 46)

- **Gluttony can lead to humiliation and poverty.**

When you sit down to eat with a ruler, consider carefully what is before you; and put a knife to your throat if you are a man given to appetite.

(Proverbs 23:1, 2)

For the drunkard and *the glutton will come to poverty,* and drowsiness will clothe a man with rags.

(Proverbs 23:21)

153

- **Gluttony is consistent with shortsightedness.**

  …lest there be any fornicator or profane person like Esau,
  who *for one morsel* of food sold his birthright.

  (Hebrews 12:16)

- **Gluttony is a mark of the absence of self-discipline.**

  Now the sons of Eli were corrupt; they did not know
  the LORD. And the priests' custom with the people
  was that when any man offered a sacrifice, the priest's
  servant would come with a three-pronged fleshhook in
  his hand while the meat was boiling. Then he would
  thrust it into the pan, or kettle, or caldron, or pot; and
  the priest would take for himself all that the fleshhook
  brought up. So they did in Shiloh to all the Israelites who
  came there. Also, before they burned the fat, the priest's
  servant would come and say to the man who sacrificed,
  "Give meat for roasting to the priest, for he will not take
  boiled meat from you, but raw." And if the man said
  to him, "They should really burn the fat first; then you
  may take as much as your heart desires," he would then
  answer him, "No, but you must *give it now*; and if not,
  I will take it by force." Therefore the sin of the young
  men was very great before the LORD, for men abhorred
  the offering of the LORD.

  (1 Samuel 2:12-17)

- **Gluttony is inconsistent for a believer's new life in
  Christ.**

  For we have spent enough of our past lifetime in doing
  the will of the Gentiles—when we walked in lewdness,
  lusts, drunkenness, revelries, drinking parties and
  abominable idolatries.

  (1 Peter 4:3)

154

BIBLICAL STEPS TOWARD
FREEDOM FROM GLUTTONY

In addition to making observations about the sin of gluttony (and it is a sin), the Bible provides life principles that will help defeat this silent, but deadly, enemy.

- **Submit to the Holy Spirit's desire to grow the fruit of self-control.**

    But the fruit of the Spirit is...self-control.

    (Galatians 5:22, 23)

    The Apostle Paul showed his commitment to mastering his appetite when he wrote: "But *I discipline my body and bring it into subjection,* lest, when I have preached to others, I myself should become disqualified."

    (1 Corinthians 9:27)

- **Give thanks to God before all meals, recognizing He has met your *needs.***

    For everything created by God is good, and nothing is to be rejected, if it is received *with gratitude;* for it is sanctified by means of the word of God and prayer.

    (1 Timothy 4:4, 5 NASB)

    On the following day, when the people who were standing on the other side of the sea saw that there was no other boat there, except that one which His disciples had entered, and that Jesus had not entered the boat with His disciples, but His disciples had gone away alone—however, other boats came from Tiberias, near the place where they ate bread *after* the Lord had given thanks.

    (John 6:22, 23)

155

So He said to them, "When you pray, say: Our Father in heaven, Hallowed be Your name. Your kingdom come. Your will be done on earth as it is in heaven. Give us day by day our daily bread."

(Luke 11:2, 3)

- **Adjust your eating habits to glorify God rather than satisfy your flesh.**

Therefore, whether you eat or drink, or whatever you do, do all to the glory of God.

(1 Corinthians 10:31)

But put on the Lord Jesus Christ, and make no provision for the flesh, to fulfill its lusts.

(Romans 13:14)

- **Pray for the Lord's strength to resist the temptation of overeating.**

Do not incline my heart to any evil thing, to practice wicked works with men who work iniquity; and do not let me eat of their delicacies.

(Psalm 141:4)

- **Recognize there is some benefit to regular exercise, though not as much as to pursuing godliness.**

For bodily exercise profits a little, but godliness is profitable for all things, having promise of the life that now is and of that which is to come.

(1 Timothy 4:8)

In other words, we must make a conscious commitment to honor God with how we care for our bodies. While in college at Yale, the great theologian, Jonathan Edwards, recognized this fact and wrote the following resolution in his diary:

> By a sparingness in diet, and eating as much as may be what is light and easy of digestion, I shall doubtless be able to think more clearly, and shall gain time; 1. By lengthening out my life; 2. Shall need less time for digestion, after meals; 3. Shall be able to study more closely, without injury to my health; 4. Shall need less time for sleep; 5. Shall more seldom be troubled with the head-ache.[47]

Not that our resolution needs to mimic Jonathan Edwards' in specifics, but we need to at least recognize that even our eating habits should be surrendered to the lordship of Christ. After all, our bodies are "for the Lord" (1 Corinthians 6:13).

CHAPTER THIRTY

When No Defense Is the Best Defense

The power of self-emptying prayer in the face of false accusation

I doubt there is any trial as painful or as difficult to endure as false accusation. External pain pales in comparison to the internal torment you feel when attacked by someone whose heart is seething with bitterness or envy towards you. How do you respond? Do you defend yourself, only to have your accuser say, "See, you *are* guilty. You would not be defending yourself if you weren't." Or is there a better alternative to self defense?

Thankfully, God's Word, as our best counselor, again comes to our rescue. I want you to notice how the response of four falsely accused men was basically the same: instead of defending themselves, they entrusted their reputations to the Lord who knew their hearts. By practicing self-emptying prayer (set in italics below), they rested in God as their Defender and the One who would vindicate them:

- **The Example of Moses (Numbers 16:1–3, 4–5; 32, 33)**

False Accusation: "Who do you think you are, Moses? We are all equal!"

Now Korah the son of Izhar, the son of Kohath, the son of Levi, with Dathan and Abiram the sons of Eliab, and On the son of Peleth, sons of Reuben, took men; and they rose up before Moses with some of the children of Israel, two hundred and fifty leaders of the congregation, representatives of the congregation, men of renown. They gathered together against Moses and Aaron, and said to them, "You take too much upon yourselves, for all the congregation is holy, every one of them, and the LORD is among them. Why then do you exalt yourselves above the assembly of the LORD?"

Response: Self-Emptying Prayer to God as Defender

So when Moses heard it, he fell on his face; and he spoke to Korah and all his company, saying, "Tomorrow morning *the LORD will show who is His* and who is holy, and will cause him to come near to Him. That one whom He chooses He will cause to come near to Him."

God's Defense:

…and the earth opened its mouth and swallowed them up, with their households and all the men with Korah, with all their goods. So they and all those with them went down alive into the pit; the earth closed over them, and they perished from among the assembly.

- **The Example Of Nehemiah (Nehemiah 6:1–9a, 9b, 10–13, 14, 16)**

False Accusation: "You are rebuilding the wall so you can be king of Jerusalem."

Now it happened when Sanballat, Tobiah, Geshem the Arab, and the rest of our enemies heard that I had rebuilt the wall, and that there were no breaks left in it (though at that time I had not hung the doors in the gates), that Sanballat and Geshem sent to me, saying, "Come, let us meet together among the villages in the plain of Ono." But they thought to do me harm. So I sent messengers to them, saying, "I am doing a great work, so that I cannot come down. Why should the work cease while I leave it and go down to you?" But they sent me this message four times, and I answered them in the same manner. Then Sanballat sent his servant to me as before, the fifth time, with an open letter in his hand. In it was written:

It is reported among the nations, and Geshem says, that you and the Jews plan to rebel; therefore, according to these rumors, you are rebuilding the wall, that you may be their king. And you have also appointed prophets to proclaim concerning you at Jerusalem, saying, "There is a king in Judah!" Now these matters will be reported to the king. So come, therefore, and let us consult together.

Then I sent to him, saying, "No such things as you say are being done, but you invent them in your own heart." For they all were trying to make us afraid, saying, "Their hands will be weakened in the work, and it will not be done."

Response: Self-Emptying Prayer to God as Defender

Now therefore, *O God, strengthen my hands.*

160

A Second, Desperate, Fear--Producing Tactic

Afterward I came to the house of Shemaiah the son of Delaiah, the son of Mehetabel, who was a secret informer; and he said, "Let us meet together in the house of God, within the temple, and let us close the doors of the temple, for they are coming to kill you; indeed, at night they will come to kill you." And I said, "Should such a man as I flee? And who is there such as I who would go into the temple to save his life? I will not go in!" Then I perceived that God had not sent him at all, but that he pronounced this prophecy against me because Tobiah and Sanballat had hired him. For this reason he was hired, that I should be afraid and act that way and sin, so that they might have cause for an evil report, that they might reproach me.

Response: Self-Emptying Prayer to God as Defender

My God, remember Tobiah and Sanballat, according to these their works, and the prophetess Noadiah and the rest of the prophets who would have made me afraid.

God's Defense:

So the wall was finished on the twenty-fifth day of Elul, in fifty-two days. And it happened, when all our enemies heard of it, and all the nations around us saw these things, that they were very disheartened in their own eyes; for they perceived that this work was done by our God.

- **The Example of Job (Job 15:1–6; 17:1–3; 42:7–8)**

False Accusation: "Face it, Job, you are guilty and full of hot air."

Then Eliphaz the Temanite answered and said: "Should a wise man answer with empty knowledge, and fill himself

161

with the east wind? Should he reason with unprofitable talk, or by speeches with which he can do no good? Yes, you cast off fear, and restrain prayer before God. For your iniquity teaches your mouth, and you choose the tongue of the crafty. Your own mouth condemns you, and not I; yes, your own lips testify against you."

Response: Self-Emptying Prayer to God as Defender

My spirit is broken, my days are extinguished, the grave is ready for me. Are not mockers with me? And does not my eye dwell on their provocation? *Now put down a pledge for me with Yourself.* Who is he who will shake hands with me?

God's Defense:

And so it was, after the LORD had spoken these words to Job, that the LORD said to Eliphaz the Temanite, "My wrath is aroused against you and your two friends, for you have not spoken of Me what is right, as My servant Job has. Now therefore, take for yourselves seven bulls and seven rams, go to My servant Job, and offer up for yourselves a burnt offering; and My servant Job shall pray for you. For I will accept him, lest I deal with you according to your folly; because you have not spoken of Me what is right, as My servant Job has."

- **The Example of Jesus (Matthew 27:13, 14; 1 Peter 2:22, 23; Philippians 2:9–11)**

False Accusation: "You call yourself a king? You are nothing more than a blaspheming carpenter's son!"

Then Pilate said to Him, "Do You not hear how many things they testify against You?" But He answered him not one word, so that the governor marveled greatly.

162

Response: Self-Emptying Prayer to God as Defender

...when He was reviled, did not revile in return; when He suffered, He did not threaten, but committed Himself to Him who judges righteously.

God's Defense:

Therefore God also has highly exalted Him and given Him the name which is above every name, that at the name of Jesus every knee should bow, of those in heaven, and of those on earth, and of those under the earth, and that every tongue should confess that Jesus Christ is Lord, to the glory of God the Father.

In the face of false accusation the easy response is to succumb to the temptation to defend ourselves, but this should be resisted. During these times, we must know the Lord will deal out justice and honor truth in *His* time, not ours, and it will be complete. We must concern ourselves more with *our own actions and attitudes* and less with those of the persons that oppose us. There is great personal benefit to be received from such painful times, but we shortchange ourselves if we give in to the fleshly tendency to fight back. The suffering the Lord sovereignly appoints for us contains purifying power and is custom-designed to stimulate our growth in Christlikeness, but it will only be gained by submitting to the Spirit's call to put on humility and the sometimes-painful practice of biblical love—loving those you do not like or those who do not like you. Entrusting our reputation and wellbeing to the only One who fully knows the truth means we must resist the temptation to defend ourselves and instead practice self-emptying prayer, placing total trust in the Lord as Judge, accompanied by an absence of desire for personal revenge. In the end, this is the only road to victory with God as our Defender.

CHAPTER THIRTY-ONE

Hope for the Homosexual

Preserving and dispensing hope
by calling sin, sin

Touted as an "alternative lifestyle," homosexuality is probably the sin getting the most attention today. It is now, for the most part, openly accepted and highly promoted throughout the media and in public education. Even churches that once adhered to God's Word have slid down the slippery slope so far as to accept, tolerate, and even promote it by officiating marriage ceremonies for people of the same sex. It is even commonplace to hear of churches ordaining homosexual men and women as ministers. However, we must ask, what does the Bible say? One of the key New Testament passages addressing homosexuality is 1 Corinthians 6:9–11.

> Do you not know that the unrighteous will not inherit the kingdom of God? Do not be deceived. Neither fornicators, nor idolaters, nor adulterers, nor homosexuals, nor sodomites, nor thieves, nor covetous, nor drunkards, nor revilers, nor extortioners will inherit the kingdom of God. And such were some of you. But you were washed, but

you were sanctified, but you were justified in the name
of the Lord Jesus and by the Spirit of our God.

Two terms are used here to denounce same-sex relations. "Homosexuals" (*malakas*), translated "effeminate"
in the King James and New American Standard Bible ver-
sions, literally means *soft*. It refers to the passive partner
in a homosexual relationship and was used of a boy kept
for homosexual relations. In Corinth, it probably referred
to the male prostitutes who made themselves available for
immoral "worship" in the temple of Aphrodite. "Sodomite"
(*arsenokoitays*) refers to the active, recruiting partner. Together, the terms describe any sexual behavior contrary to
God's original intention of one man with one woman in the
context of marriage. It includes such things as transvestism
and sex-change operations and denounces the blurring of
gender roles so prevalent in our American society.

The Bible describes the origin of the term *sodomy* in
Genesis, chapters 18 and 19. These chapters contain the his-
torical record of God's wrath against this sexual perversion.
God said to Abraham: "The outcry of Sodom and Gomorrah
is indeed great, and their sin is exceedingly grave" (18:20
NASB). As a result God showed His displeasure by raining
fire and brimstone from heaven, destroying the two cities.
So prevalent was the sin of homosexuality in that area that
the term *sodomite* was born. In his book, *Biblical Solutions
to Contemporary Problems,* Rus Walton writes of the destructive consequences of this sin:

> Sodomy promotes idolatry, invites false gods, and nur-
> tures apostasies. It spawns additional perversions; it
> gnaws at the vitals and rots the soul—first, the souls
> of those who indulge in its lusts and evils and, ulti-
> mately, the soul of the nation that permits it to continue

unchallenged. Historically, rampant homosexuality has been one of the social malignancies that preceded the fall of nations and empires. (Greece, Rome, etc)[48]

God's Word unequivocally condemns homosexuality for the three reasons here stated, but also always offers the hope of forgiveness to those who repent:

1. Homosexuality is abominable.

Leviticus 18:22 says, "You shall not lie with a male as with a woman. It is an abomination." God views same-sex relations not as a different form of "love," but as a distortion of the beauty of His original plan. The Bible describes these actions in enough detail to reveal exactly what God condemns, but not too much so as to pollute minds unnecessarily. Some Christian ministries believe it is their calling to *expose them* in detail by directing attention to books and Internet sites that promote various perversions. However, the very next verse warns: "...it is shameful even to speak of those things which are done by them in secret" (Ephesians 5:11, 12). It seems to me Paul's counsel to the Romans must also be heeded: "For your obedience has become known to all. Therefore I am glad on your behalf; but I want you to be wise in what is good, and *simple concerning evil*" (Romans 16:19). Somewhere between the obligation to *expose them* and to remain *simple concerning evil* lies a balance of wisdom and discretion.

2. Homosexuality is rebellious.

But we know that the law is good if one uses it lawfully, knowing this: that the law is not made for a righteous person, but for the lawless and insubordinate, for the ungodly and for sinners, for the unholy and profane, for murderers of fathers and murderers of mothers, for manslayers, for fornicators, for sodomites, for kidnappers, for liars, for perjurers, and if there is any other thing that is contrary to sound doctrine.

(1 Timothy 1:8–10)

God gave His law to protect His people from the destruction of sin and to expose the wickedness of man's heart, thus ushering in the hope, freedom, and forgiveness found only in Jesus Christ. When men redefine homosexuality as a disease or a genetic disorder, instead of calling it *sin*, hope is stolen from those who need it most. It is *not* always God's will that men be healed of diseases, but it *is* always His will we be delivered from our rebellion.

3. Homosexuality is unnatural.

The first chapter of Romans describes the degeneration of man, the downward spiral people naturally ride when they forget God; specifically, when they know God, but do not honor Him as such. The spiral begins: ". . . although they knew God, they did not glorify Him as God, nor were thankful, but became futile in their thoughts, and their foolish hearts were darkened" (1:21). Rejection of God produces a darkened mind, which leads to idolatry. As a result, God gives men over, i.e., He pulls out all the stops and lets them become in their lives what they already are in their hearts. This sin is not exclusive to men, either:

For this reason God gave them up to vile passions. For even their women exchanged the natural use for what is against nature. Likewise also the men, leaving the natural use of the woman, burned in their lust for one another, men with men committing what is shameful, and receiving in themselves the penalty of their error which was due. (1:26, 27)

Homosexuality is unnatural because it defies God's original plan in creation. "So God created man in His own image; in the image of God He created him; *male and female He created them*" (Genesis 1:27).

4. Homosexuality is forgivable.

The Bible also brings hope to the homosexual by honestly naming his or her lust and behavior *sin*, thus opening the door to the Gospel. Jesus died *for sin* in order to cleanse and break us free from its grip and make us right with God. He did not come to call the righteous, but *sinners* (Matthew 9:13). The hope of 1 Corinthians 6:11 is in the word *were*. "And such *were* some of you. But you *were* washed, but you *were* sanctified, but you *were* justified in the name of the Lord Jesus and by the Spirit of our God." The church at Corinth contained former homosexuals, men and women who had been washed clean by God. This is the power of the Gospel and the marvelous story of what the Spirit of God does when He saves a sinner. Ed Welch writes:

An effective church should have homosexuals! Because of the love of Christ, the church should pursue homosexuals. And through its exaltation of Christ in preaching, corporate prayer, and worship, the church should attract homosexuals. It should minister the Word to those who are already in church by flushing out the self-deceived, exposing the dishonest, confronting the rebel, offering forgiveness to the guilt-ridden, and giving hope. The church should also welcome those who struggle with homosexuality but have never been part of the church. The church should surprise them with love, a sense of family, and the absence of self-righteous judgment. It should offer truth in a way that is convicting, attractive, and radically different from anything else the homosexual has ever heard. May God enable us to fulfill this high calling.[49]

We will be faithful to this calling not by following the politically correct language and agenda of the world, but by upholding what the Bible says about homosexuality, by speaking forth what God says. To call homosexual behavior anything other than a ruinous deviation from God's original plan for sexuality is to undermine the precious work of the life-changing Gospel of Jesus Christ. It is also less than helpful to tell someone struggling with homosexual desires something like this:

> You are in many ways a victim of circumstance. As far as the development of your attraction to the same sex is concerned, you're blameless. God does not and will not hold that against you. It is not a sin to be homosexually inclined [i.e., to have homosexual desires]. It's what you do with those inclinations that condemns or commends you.[50]

Surely Jesus would not agree with this statement. If a man who lusts after a woman is guilty of committing adultery in his heart (Matthew 5:28), surely he would incur the same guilt if it were same-sex lust. Desires are sinful even when they do not produce corresponding actions.

169

"You desire truth in the *inward* parts," the Scripture says (Psalm 51:6). A more biblically accurate view is:

> ... it is possible that the church has accepted the unbiblical category of homosexual orientation because it has misunderstood the nature of sin. Sin has been reduced to mature, rational, conscious decisions. Perhaps the church has lost sight of the fact that sin is far more than that. It is part of our human fabric, and it works on a deep and quiet level....the church must warn and rebuke those who call themselves Christians but persist in homosexual practice, *and* the church must actively teach that homosexual affection is sinful. There is no morally neutral, in-born, homosexual orientation. To tell those struggling with homosexual desire to simply refrain from acting on it is to sin against these brothers and sisters.[51]

By calling sin *sin*, we offer unbelievers the hope of deliverance through the Gospel and assure the Christian who has been delivered, but remains tempted, that God's grace will continue to empower him to remain victorious over the control of sin and strengthen him on the road of obedience as he daily submits to the Word of God.

> Now to Him who is able to keep you from stumbling, and to present you faultless before the presence of His glory with exceeding joy, to God our Savior, Who alone is wise, be glory and majesty, dominion and power, both now and forever. Amen.
>
> (Jude 24, 25)

CHAPTER THIRTY-TWO

Lessening the Pain of Divine Discipline Without Getting in God's Way

Helping mercy and truth "kiss" each other

t is *not* difficult to know how to help a brother in material need when the cause of the need is some kind of unforeseen tragedy—like a fire that burns down a house or a factory layoff resulting in unemployment. The obvious response is to rally together and leave no need unmet (Acts 4:34; 1 John 3:17; James 2:15, 16). However, it is another thing altogether to discern how to help when it is most probable that the need has been caused by lack of sound judgment, rebellion against God's ways, foolish or rash decisions, or failure to seek a multitude of counselors. In this case, it is essential to avoid interfering with God's most frequently used tool of correction: the Law of the Harvest (Galatians 6:7). If by his reaping what is sown God is able to get an erring believer's attention more effectively and readily than by other means, are we not getting in His way when we alleviate painful consequences?

This is the challenge of ministering to hurting people in a fallen world; of striking a delicate balance for the sake of healing, spiritual growth, and restoration; of showing mercy without compromising biblical truth. "Let not mercy and truth forsake you; bind them around your neck, write them on the tablet of your heart, and so find favor and high esteem in the sight of God and man" (Proverbs 3:3, 4). God intended for mercy and truth to work together as two sides of the same coin; that they be bound around our necks *together*...the result being favor in the sight of God *and* man. In other words, when applying truth to a fellow brother's need, it is crucial that it be done in a spirit of kindness for the sake of the goal of spiritual restoration. In so doing, God is pleased and a brother is truly helped. In this, God is our example. Hebrews 12:4–11 is clear in its presentation of the restorative discipline of God:

> You have not yet resisted to bloodshed, striving against sin. And you have forgotten the exhortation which speaks to you as to sons: "My son, do not despise the chastening of the LORD, nor be discouraged when you are rebuked by Him; for whom the LORD loves He chastens, and scourges every son whom He receives." If you endure chastening, God deals with you as with sons; for what son is there whom a father does not chasten? But if you are without chastening, of which all have become partakers, then you are illegitimate and not sons. Furthermore, we have had human fathers who corrected us, and we paid them respect. Shall we not much more readily be in subjection to the Father of spirits and live? For they indeed for a few days chastened us as seemed best to them, but He for our profit, that we may be partakers of His holiness. Now no chastening seems to be joyful for the present, but painful; nevertheless, afterward it yields the peaceable fruit of righteousness to those who have been trained by it.

From this passage, five principles emerge:

1. Discipline is a mark of the commitment of God's love toward His children (vs. 5).
2. The absence of discipline in the life of a sinning Christian calls his relationship with God into question (vv. 7, 8).
3. God disciplines His children so we will be restored and grow in holiness (vs. 10).
4. Discipline is painful, not joyful (vs. 11a).
5. Discipline brings great benefit to those who are willing to let it be their *trainer-in-righteousness* (vs. 11b).

I taught the above passage numerous times before I saw the connection with the verses that follow:

> Therefore strengthen the hands which hang down, and the feeble knees, and make straight paths for your feet, so that what is lame may not be dislocated, but rather be healed.
>
> (Hebrews 12:12, 13)

"Therefore" is there for a reason—to make us look at the preceding thought. In this case, it is to call attention to the role of a body of believers toward its members who may be enduring the chastening hand of God. Our ministry toward those in our church who suffer due to their own choices must be a blend of practical acts of kindness, which bring encouragement ("strengthen the hands which hang down, and the feeble knees"), and biblical counsel that will guide them back onto God's straight and narrow path and hopefully prevent future error ("make straight paths...so that what is lame may...be healed").

173

Individual believers and churches usually err in one of two extremes: they either smother the discipline of God in a blanket of sentimental "love" by easing the pain without addressing the cause of the sin-wound, or they hold to the truth in such a harsh, rigid way that mercy is virtually non-existent. What is so desperately needed is the preservation of the marriage of *kindness* and *truth* so that the erring one is not punished for stepping off God's path, but gently restored to the road of obedience that leads to righteousness. When this approach is taken, "Mercy and truth have met together; righteousness and peace have kissed" (Psalm 85:10).

CHAPTER THIRTY-THREE

The Power of Encouragement

Lessons from a "forgotten servant"

Have you ever experienced the power of encourage-ment? I can remember many times over the years when God provided faithful believers who were "others-focused" enough to come alongside and strengthen my hands for His work. The Apostle Paul had such a man by his side, by the name of Onesiphorus. He is one of the "forgotten servants" in the biblical record. His name says it all. Onesiphorus means, "profit bringer," and that is exactly what he was. As Paul sat in a Roman prison, consider-ing the last words he would pen under the inspiration of the Holy Spirit, the name of his faithful friend could not help but come to mind. Here we learn three qualities of a faithful encourager:

- **An encourager dispenses refreshing motivation in the midst of ministerial rejection.**

"This you know, that all those in Asia have turned away from me, among whom are Phygellus and Hermogenes.

The Lord grant mercy to the household of Onesiphorus, for he often refreshed me, and was not ashamed of my chain" (2 Timothy 1:15, 16). As a preacher of the biblical Gospel and the whole counsel of God, Paul was accustomed to abandonment. Like Jesus, he had many people who wanted to come along for the ride, but when commitment to the ways of God and the Word of God meant discomfort and even persecution, the crowd departed and he was left with a faithful few.

Onesiphorus was one of those faithful servants who *refreshed* Paul. This is the only occurrence of the word *refreshed* in the New Testament. It paints a picture of one who provides a cool refreshing breeze for one about to faint. Our day is not much different than the one in which Paul lived. Many are looking for a free ride and will "follow" Jesus, until disappointment walks through their door or dying to self becomes a harsh reality. May God develop in each of us the perseverance required to be a faithful dispenser of encouragement to others over the long-haul.

- **An encourager devotes himself to the refreshment of others with great eagerness.**

Verse 17 says, "but when he arrived in Rome, he sought me out very zealously and found me." Onesiphorus did not sit around waiting or even praying for opportunities to serve. As soon as he learned of a need he acted on it, even if it meant searching a Roman prison to find his brother. We must not allow our ministry mindset to be dictated by our "culture of convenience." Being a faithful encourager requires that we be people of initiative

176

who *search out* ways to refresh other believers, even if it means personal sacrifice or inconvenience.

• **An encourager displays loyalty in the face of adversity.**

Adversity has a way of revealing who your true friends really are. In contrast to all who were in Asia that turned away from Paul, Onesiphorus was "not ashamed" of Paul's imprisonment (1:16). He knew the meaning of Proverbs 17:17: "A friend loves at all times." Later, Paul wrote, "At my first defense no one stood with me, but all forsook me" (2 Timothy 4:16). Yet three verses later, he asked Timothy to greet Onesiphorus (4:19). His courageous spirit and devotion to Paul stood in stark contrast to the infidelity of so many others. Being a faithful encourager requires loyalty that endures through difficult times.

The refreshing example of Onesiphorus is worthy of imitation. May God grant us grace to be "others-focused" so that fellow believers around us may truly experience the power of encouragement.

CHAPTER THIRTY-FOUR

When War Is Just

*Sometimes loving our enemies means going
to war against them*

If we are commanded to love our enemies, why do so many Christians continue to support our President's actions against Iraq? Doesn't our support contradict such mandates as: "Overcome evil with good" (Romans 12:21), and "Love does no harm to a neighbor" (Romans 13:10)? What counsel does God's Word offer?

When it comes to the subject of war, Christians have historically been divided into two positions: "pacifist" and "just war." The pacifist interprets some teachings of Jesus in such a way as to conclude that war is always wrong and, therefore, it is not right for a Christian to be involved in it or to support it. The *just war* position views war as a necessary evil due to the greater evil, man himself, who is responsible for it. The difference between the two views hinges primarily on differing interpretations of the following portion of the Sermon on the Mount:

"You have heard that it was said, 'An eye for an eye and a tooth for a tooth.' But I tell you not to resist an evil person. But whoever slaps you on your right cheek, turn the other to him also. If anyone wants to sue you and take away your tunic, let him have your cloak also. And whoever compels you to go one mile, go with him two. Give to him who asks you, and from him who wants to borrow from you do not turn away. You have heard that it was said, 'You shall love your neighbor and hate your enemy.' But I say to you, love your enemies, bless those who curse you, do good to those who hate you, and pray for those who spitefully use you and persecute you, that you may be sons of your Father in heaven; for He makes His sun rise on the evil and on the good, and sends rain on the just and on the unjust."

(Matthew 5:38–45)

Historically, this Scripture has been used by such leaders and groups as William Penn, the Mennonites, and the Quakers to promote their pacifist tradition of nonviolence. However, an accurate interpretation of this passage depends on the answer to one question: "Is Jesus teaching against national vengeance or personal revenge?" Clearly the emphasis of the context is on individuals, *not* nations. Individuals have cheeks and shirts, not nations. Individuals walk miles. Nations do not. Jesus is definitely commanding a God-honoring substitute for personal revenge.

John Jefferson Davis has done the Church an enormous favor by writing *Evangelical Ethics*,[52] in which he aptly explains why this passage cannot be used to support the position of nonviolence where nations are concerned:

As a private individual, considering only my own interests and standing before God, I may choose to literally turn the other cheek in the face of unjust aggression. When I stand in a relation of guardianship to third parties, as a civil magistrate, a parent, or a husband, however,

179

then the responsibilities of Christian love have a different application. Because of my love for those under my care, and out of concern for their lives and welfare, I must resist unjust aggression against them. Love of my neighbor does not mean standing idly by when my wife is being brutally raped; it means using whatever force is necessary to protect her life and safety. My divine obligation to provide for the needs of my own family (1 Timothy 5:8) certainly includes, as an irreducible minimum, protecting them from deadly assault. (p. 213)

The pacifist is right in believing God is a God of peace, but forgets He is also a God of war. The pacifist also fails to acknowledge that God knows human nature too well to think such a thing as world peace is possible before His Son returns to set up His kingdom—a kingdom of peace brought about by justice.

"There will be a time when swords will finally be turned into plowshares, but in the interim, the demands of divine justice and love of the neighbor sometimes require the use of force in the legitimate defense of innocent human life" (p. 213). In other words, it is not only justice that demands punishment of evil, but love that pursues the protection of the innocent.

However, "In the pacifist understanding, if one finds oneself in a situation in which it seems impossible to preserve both the values of justice and of nonviolence, then one chooses nonviolence, even at the price of allowing great injustices to be perpetrated upon oneself and innocent third parties" (p. 211). But is this really *love?* If love does what is in the best interest of its neighbor, is it really love to allow the torture of the innocent to continue unchecked? The answer to that question stresses the importance of having a biblical view of love. Davis warns:

An emphasis on love to the exclusion of the sterner dimensions of God's wrath and justice soon leads to a concept of love that is sentimental and humanistic, quite different from that revealed in Scripture....By restraining an evil aggressor, even through deadly force, one can act in love, because in so doing one can reduce the eternal weight of guilt for which the aggressor will have to answer. Love acts with the enemy's eternal welfare in view, and it is in no one's interest to compound an eternal weight of guilt. (p. 218)

In other words, it is not only loving to protect those who are being treated unjustly, but it is also loving to stop the guilty one from building his heap of evil deeds higher, thus incurring more judgment.

Therefore, the *just war* position understands that war has been, and will continue to be, used by God to judge nations. It is crucial for us to remember the God-ordained purpose of government to punish evil and reward good. It is "God's minister" that "does not bear the sword in vain" (Romans 13:3, 4a). Therefore, to embark upon dethroning a cold-blooded tyrant like Saddam Hussein is to perform a heroic act of justice that in the end promotes genuine peace; it is using our national power to protect others who are weaker and unable to defend themselves.

But, you ask, does this principle mean one nation has the *right* to judge another? Perhaps the better question is: does *God* have a right to use one nation to punish another? I say this with caution because we do not know the mind of God, but is it possible that the United States could be used as, "an avenger to execute wrath on him who practices evil" (Romans 13:4b)?

For God to use one nation to judge another does not necessarily mean that the instrumental nation is righteous.

Babylon was God's chosen instrument of judgment on Israel (Book of Jeremiah) and Nineveh (Book of Nahum), yet it was ruthlessly wicked. Though Nebuchadnezzar was an evil leader, God called him, "My servant" (Jeremiah 27:6, 43:10). So, it would be incorrect for us to think the United States has a right to punish other nations because we are "more righteous." That is not the issue at all. The issue is: God raises and lowers world leaders and nations for His sovereign purposes (Daniel 2:21). Could the President of the United States have been raised up as an instrument of God to lower another? The Bible answers in the affirmative.

As horrible as war is, there is something more evil: standing by and idly watching millions of *neighbors* continue to be tormented and afflicted. It seems to me the *just war* theory is most consistent with the whole counsel of God found in the Scriptures. Davis concludes:

> The just war tradition, then, attempts to place the emphasis where Scripture itself does: when the values of justice and nonviolence conflict in a fallen world, the vindication of divine standards of justice takes precedence. The cross of Jesus Christ is the demonstration of God's own vindication of justice (Romans 3:25, 26), even at the terrible cost of violence directed against His own Son. Those who truly desire peace must be willing to defend life against those who would destroy it unjustly. (p. 218)

I am convinced that at this point in history God has chosen to use America to judge a nation more wicked than herself and to free millions of afflicted and tormented people. I believe the current conflicts in Iraq and Afghanistan are biblically defensible as just wars, and that it is our duty as Christians to continue to support and pray for our military and national leaders.

CHAPTER THIRTY-FIVE

When "Grace" Becomes a License to Live in Sin

Jude tried to warn me about debates in the church foyer

"Will you die in your sin?" That was the question the *foyer debater* threw in my face as he became increasingly indignant over my remaining unmoved by his arguments. With great energy, he strove to convince me that all Christians will go to heaven, but not all will be allowed into the heavenly city; that all Christians will inherit eternal life, but not all will inherit the Kingdom. Apparently, according to his belief, obedient Christians will enjoy city life while those Christians who "die in their sin" will have to live in the country. In other words, a "Christian" can be a libertine as long as he is content to live in the suburbs.

At first glance he appeared to be just another visitor to our church, but it wasn't long before his real agenda was revealed as he tried to proselytize a few of the immature with his false doctrine. Even this was simply a masquerade for a cocky young man looking for a fight.

His point in asking the question was to challenge my doctrinal view that true believers in Christ cannot live in a constant, habitual state of sin without incurring divine discipline, a view based on the teaching of 1 John, which states that, "whoever is born of God does not sin" [present tense: continuous sinning]; "but He who has been born of God keeps himself, and the wicked one does not touch him" (1 John 5:18), and Hebrews, "But if you are without chastening, of which all have become partakers, then you are illegitimate and not sons" (Hebrews 12:8). In light of passages like these, the question is not, "Will you *die* in your sin?" but, "Can a true Christian perpetually *live* in sin?"

You see, one of the marks of a false teacher is the inconsistency of his teachings. In this case, the website promoted on the young man's literature contains articles sharply accusing John MacArthur, Jr., of teaching a "false Gospel" because he believes, as I do, that genuine saving faith will demonstrate itself by good works and progressive godliness in the life of the believer.

Upon closer inspection, it seems the website also contains numerous articles performing all kinds of mental gymnastics to purport that the Bible prescribes certain hairstyles for men, absolutely forbids a woman from wearing pants, and promotes the insupportable notion that there is only one true Bible translation. The end result is that he himself is guilty of teaching *works righteousness,* the very thing he accuses others of doing! "Works righteousness" feeds the flesh by making an outward *form* of holiness attainable solely by human effort. For example, it is much easier to tell women they cannot wear pants than it is to tell them to wear a meek and quiet spirit. And it is infinitely easier to get men to cut their hair to a certain length than it is to help them forsake lust.

The only explanation for this baffling combination of works righteousness and "grace" is what Jude, the apostle, warned of. That is, false teachers often craft their doctrine in such a way so as to *retain* their ungodly lifestyles.

> Beloved, while I was making every effort to write you about our common salvation, I felt the necessity to write to you appealing that you contend earnestly for the faith which was once for all delivered to the saints. For certain persons have crept in unnoticed, those who were long beforehand marked out for this condemnation, *ungodly persons who turn the grace of our God into licentiousness* and *deny our only Master and Lord,* Jesus Christ.
>
> (Jude 3, 4 NASB)

According to Jude and other New Testament writers, false teachers have three terribly bad habits. First, they are often ungodly in their own behavior and, therefore, alter biblical grace to fit their licentious lifestyles. When this happens, escape routes are invented to give false assurance to ungodly "Christians," thus acres of land are developed outside the heavenly city; the suburbs of heaven are built.

Second, they deny the lordship of Christ. Here, Peter agrees with Jude: "But there were also false prophets among the people, even as there will be false teachers among you, who will secretly bring in destructive heresies, *even denying the Lord who bought them,* and bring on themselves swift destruction" (2 Peter 2:1).

Third, they replace biblical submission of the heart and will with a self-prescribed list of "spiritual" regulations that can easily be obeyed without the power of the Spirit. "But know this, that in the last days perilous times will come: for men will be...lovers of pleasure rather than lovers of God, having a *form of godliness* but denying its power. And from such people turn away" (2 Timothy 3:1, 2, 4, 5)!

185

So the question is not, "Will we *die* in our sin?" but, "Will we continue to *live* in our sin?" *May it never be!* Grace is not a free license to live as we please, but rather, divine incentive and empowerment for holiness. "For the grace of God that brings salvation has appeared to all men, teaching us that, denying ungodliness and worldly lusts, we should live soberly, righteously, and godly in the present age" (Titus 2:11, 12).

CHAPTER THIRTY-SIX

The Dangers of Excessive Talk

Learning to tame your tongue

Is it a sin to talk too much? Well, that depends. In our men's group earlier this week we discussed the discipline of the tongue. After reading a chapter in *Disciplines of a Godly Man*[33] and verses from Proverbs that address the issue, some of us were tempted to stop talking all together! However, we quickly realized this was not the answer. That would be too easy. The right response is the hard road of self-discipline. The hard road is the application of wisdom in the restraint of the most powerful muscle in our body. That got me thinking about the dangers of talking too much. There are many, and include the following:

- **Excessive talk may open the door to sin.**

  "In the multitude of words sin is not lacking, but he who restrains his lips is wise" (Proverbs 10:19). "Whoever guards his mouth and tongue keeps his soul from troubles" (21:23). "He who guards his mouth preserves his life, but he who opens wide his lips shall have destruction" (13:3). These verses seem to be saying the more you talk, the more you will sin. The reason for this is found in the sobering truth of James 3:8: "But no man can tame the tongue. It is an unruly evil, full of deadly poison." We must discipline ourselves to refrain from speaking when it is not necessary. This is one mark of wisdom. "He who has knowledge spares his words, and a man of understanding is of a calm spirit. Even a fool is counted wise when he holds his peace; when he shuts his lips, he is considered perceptive" (17:27, 28).

- **Excessive talk may fuel gossip.**

  Webster's Dictionary defines a gossip as, "a person who chatters or repeats idle talk and rumors."[54] So, idle talk and rumors define the content of gossip. However, it is important to realize that the accuracy of the information being chattered about is not the issue. It could be true or false. The issue is there are some things that simply don't need to be, and should not be, *repeated* because the negative effects of gossip are numerous. It destroys friendships: "He who covers a transgression seeks love, but he who repeats a matter separates friends" (Proverbs 17:9). It causes strife: "Where there is no wood, the fire goes out; and where there is no talebearer, strife ceases" (Proverbs 26:20). It leads to the betrayal of confidences: "He who goes about as a slanderer reveals secrets, therefore do not associate with a gossip" (Proverbs 20:19 NASB). It hurts others deeply: "The words of a talebearer are like tasty trifles, and they go down into the inmost body" (Proverbs 18:8). The Puritan, Thomas Watson, said: "The scorpion carries its poison in its tail, the slanderer in his tongue. His words pierce deep like the quills of the porcupine."[55]

- **Excessive talk may be the enemy of listening.**

  I am sure we have all been guilty at one time or another of *not listening* because we were rapidly forming a response in our mind while the other person was still talking. Proverbs identifies this as foolishness: "He who answers a matter before he hears it, it is folly and shame to him" (18:13). "Do you see a man hasty in his words? There is more hope for a fool than for him" (29:20). This is also supported by the words of James in the New Testament: "Let every man be swift to hear, slow to speak" (James. 1:19). Notice the relationship between quick listening and slow speaking. It seems the discipline of *quick listening* strengthens the discipline of *slow speaking*, and vice versa. So, if I make a conscious decision to listen intently, I will not be so hasty to speak. And if I use more care in speaking, I will become a more skillful listener.

- **Excessive talk may feed boasting.**

  To boast is to glory in having or doing something. Boasters are different from gossips in that they talk excessively about themselves rather than others. Proverbs warns against this: "Let another man praise you, and not your own mouth; a stranger, and not your own lips" (27:2). "Most men will proclaim each his own goodness, but who can find a faithful man?" (20:6) "Whoever falsely boasts of giving is like clouds and wind without rain" (25:14). Boasting is grievous to God because it is fueled by pride. We need to carefully heed James' warning:

  Come now, you who say, "Today or tomorrow we will go to such and such a city, spend a year there, buy and

189

sell, and make a profit;" whereas you do not know what will happen tomorrow. For what is your life? It is even a vapor that appears for a little time and then vanishes away. Instead you ought to say, "If the Lord wills, we shall live and do this or that." But now you boast in your arrogance. All such boasting is evil.

(James 4:13–16)

- **Excessive talk may lead to flattery.**

It would be foolish to try to improve on Kent Hughes' definition of flattery: "Gossip involves saying behind a person's back what you would never say to his or her face. Flattery means saying to a person's face what you would never say behind his or her back."[56] The Bible always attributes corrupt motives to flattery. "A man who flatters his neighbor spreads a net for his feet" (Proverbs 29:5). The harlot seduces her prey by means of flattery (Proverbs 2:16–18, 6:24, 7:21). In the past when I have encountered a flatterer, I have wanted to ask, "Just what is it you want?" Beware of those who give excessive, untrue, or insincere praise.

- **Excessive talk may be idle talk.**

If we fail to restrain the use of our tongue, we may find ourselves involved in a lot of useless talk. Proverbs 14:23 says, "In all labor there is profit, but idle chatter leads only to poverty." In other words, *all talk and no action* eventually leads to want. Jesus' warning against idle talk should have a sobering effect: "But I say to you that for every idle word men may speak, they will give account of it in the day of judgment" (Matthew 12:36). The accounting we shall give at the Judgment Seat of Christ is a powerful deterrent to careless speech if we will heed it.

- **Excessive talk may give birth to profanity.**

Profanity, or what most of us grew up calling "swearing," is inconsistent in the life of a child of God. "With [the tongue] we bless our Lord and Father; and with it we curse men, who have been made in the likeness of God; from the same mouth come both blessing and cursing" (James 3:9, 10a NASB). If we sing praise to God on Sunday and curse men on Monday, "My brethren, these things ought not to be this way" (James 3:10 NASB). "It is inconsistent for a fountain to send out from the same opening both fresh and bitter water, or a fig tree to produce olives" (James 3:11, 12). Therefore, our *new-creature-status* in Christ should be reflected by the abandonment of profane talk (2 Corinthians 5:17).

- **Excessive talk may destroy many.**

"Even so the tongue is a little member and boasts great things. See how great a forest a little fire kindles! And *the tongue is a fire,* a world of iniquity. The tongue is so set among our members that it defiles the whole body, and sets on fire the course of nature; and it is set on fire by hell" (James 3:5, 6). The National Interagency Fire Center reports that in the year 2000 fires destroyed 8,422,237 acres of wildland, costing federal agencies (us) over 1.3 billion dollars to suppress.[57] We can measure the destruction of trees and wildlife, but the devastation caused by an uncontrolled tongue cannot be estimated. Just one spark is all it takes!

Taming our tongue is extremely difficult, but not impossible. As we exercise discipline in the restraint of our tongue, the Holy Spirit will produce the fruit of *self-control*

(Galatians 5:23). As we grow in the grace and knowledge of the Lord Jesus, we will become more and more like the *perfect* (complete, mature) man who does not *stumble in word* (James 3:2). Let us pray we become more like that man.

CHAPTER THIRTY-SEVEN

How to be a *Great* Grandparent

Using your influence for the cause of Christ

Never underestimate your influence on the faith and spiritual growth of your grandchildren. It was because of the faithful and loving witness of a grandmother that our hymnals bulge with the poetry of Fanny Crosby. In her day, Fanny Crosby was considered the greatest hymn writer in America. In his biography, Bernard Ruffin states:

> Johann Strauss reigned as the waltz king of Vienna, and John Philip Sousa the march king of Washington; Fanny Crosby reigned as the hymn queen in New York during the latter nineteenth and early twentieth centuries. Charles H. Gabriel (1856–1932), himself a noted hymn writer and author of several popular songs, at her death lamented the loss of the woman whose "name, suspended as a halo above modern hymnology...[she] will live on as long as people sing the Gospel."[58]

Kenneth Osbeck, author of several books on hymnology, wrote:

> In the period of 1870 to her death in 1915, it is estimated that Fanny Crosby wrote between 8,000 and 9,000 Gospel hymn texts, more than any other known hymn writer. The majority of her lasting favorites were written in her midlife during the decade of the 1870s. These include such popular hymns still found in our hymnals as "Safe in the Arms of Jesus," "Blessed Assurance," "Pass Me Not, 'O Gentle Savior," "Jesus, Keep Me Near the Cross," "I Am Thine, O Lord," "All the Way My Savior Leads Me," "Close to Thee," "Praise Him, Praise Him!" "To God Be the Glory," and "Rescue the Perishing."[59]

While still an infant, barely six-weeks-old, Fanny was afflicted with an infection that inflamed her eyes. When the family doctor could not be found, a quack applied a hot poultice to her eyes, burning the corneas and causing scar tissue to form. The result was a loss of all vision, except for the ability to barely distinguish between light and dark. But it is not Fanny Crosby, the blind hymn writer, I ask you to remember right now, but her grandmother. For without the influence of this godly woman, we may have never been blessed with so many great hymns.

- *Great* **grandparents pray** *for* **and** *with* **their grand-children.**

Fanny Crosby's father died unexpectedly when she was only nine months old. Her mother, Mercy, a widow at twenty-one, hired herself out to a wealthy farmer as a maidservant and Fanny's grandmother became her primary caregiver. Fanny attributed much of what she became to the influence of her godly grandmother who, by example, taught her how to pray and trust God. In her autobiography, she writes:

My grandmother was a woman of exemplary piety and from her I learned many useful and abiding lessons. She was a firm believer in prayer; and, when I was very young, taught me to believe that our Father in heaven will always give us whatever is for our good; and therefore that we should be careful not to ask him anything that is not consistent with his holy will. At evening-time she used to call me to her dear old rocking chair; then we would kneel down together and repeat some simple petition (pp. 15, 16).[60]

One evening when she was ten years old, Fanny was especially discouraged because the local schoolteacher did not have personal time for her. Of that night, she wrote:

Toward twilight she [grandma] called me to her and both of us sat for a time talking in the old rocking chair. Then we knelt down by its side and repeated a petition to the kind Father, after which she went quietly down the stairs, leaving me alone with my own thoughts. (p. 37)

As she knelt by the window, Fanny prayed, "Dear Lord, please show me how I can learn like other children." She later shared, "At this moment the weight of anxiety that had burdened my heart was changed to the sweet consciousness that my prayer would be answered in due time" (p. 37). *Grandparents, teach your little ones how to pray!*

• *Great* **grandparents balance affection with firmness.**

Too many grandparents are proud of how they, "spoil the grandchildren and send them home." No doubt we all fondly remember our grandparents for "spoiling" us a little; however, Christian grandparents must be careful not to abandon firm discipline when it is appropriate for them to administer it. After her grandmother died, Fanny composed this poem about her loving affection:

> *In her loving arms she held me,*
> *And beneath her patient care,*
> *I was borne away to dreamland*
> *In her dear, old rocking chair.*

However, in addition to ample amounts of affection, her grandmother modeled the loving discipline of the heavenly Father. Fanny wrote, "[Grandma] was always kind, though firm; and never punished me for ordinary offenses; on the contrary, she would talk to me very gently, and in this way she would convince me of my fault and bring me into a state of real and heartfelt penitence" (p. 16). This wise grandmother did not ignore disobedience or simply scold her granddaughter for doing something wrong, but carefully used truth to appeal to her conscience and bring her to true repentance. By doing so, she was not undermining, but rather reinforcing the discipline already being administered by the child's mother. *Grandparents, love your little ones with much affection and much firmness!*

- *Great* **grandparents pass on their faith by example and instruction.**

No doubt the greatest biblical example of a godly grandparent is that of Lois, grandmother of the young pastor, Timothy. "For I am mindful of the sincere faith within you, which first dwelt in your grandmother Lois, and your mother Eunice, and I am sure that it is in you as well" (2 Timothy 1:5 NASB). This faith was taught by word and modeled by deed. "You, however, continue in the things you have learned and become convinced of, *knowing from whom you have learned them; and that from childhood you have known the sacred writings* which are able to give you the wisdom that leads to salvation through faith which is in Christ Jesus" (2 Timothy 3:14, 15 NASB). The sacred writings are, of course, the God-breathed Scriptures mentioned in the next verse. The Holy Spirit used the Scriptures as they were consistently taught by Timothy's mother and grandmother to lead him to repentance and faith in Jesus Christ. What greater reward could a grandparent receive? *Grandparents, pass on your Christian faith through a godly example and biblical instruction!*

Christian grandparents, you are an important part of God's plan to cultivate young disciples of Jesus Christ. Seize your opportunity to influence the younger generations for Him. May God richly bless you as you wisely use your influence.

CHAPTER THIRTY-EIGHT

The Proverbs Plan

A simple strategy for daily devotions

D o you ever struggle being consistent in your daily devotions? Do you sometimes wonder, "Where in the Bible should I read today? Should I read in the Old Testament or the New? Should I read Psalms or Isaiah? Or, maybe I should start in Genesis and just keep reading until I finish Revelation." Or do you play *Bible Roulette,* close your eyes, fan the pages of your Bible, and then stop. Wherever you land *must* be where God wants you to read today, right?

Well, as a fellow-struggler in the quest for a disciplined life, let me share a simple plan I have turned to from time to time, which has led to considerable success. I don't remember where the suggestion first came from, but it is not original with me. Sometime in the past someone recommended a simple plan for getting into the Word of God daily. For lack of a better name, I call it *The Proverbs Plan.* One of the reasons it leads to quick success is you can start this plan at any time. You don't have to wait until New Year's Day to make a resolution and start a new habit. "Experts" (whoever they are) have long claimed that it takes about thirty days to form a new habit. Perfect! *The Proverbs Plan* takes advantage of the fact that there are thirty-one chapters in the book and thirty-one days in most of our months.

This is how it works. If today is the fifth day of the month, read chapter five. Tomorrow, read chapter six, and so on. If you miss a day, you can read two chapters the next day or skip the one you missed and read it when it comes up next month. In months that have less than thirty-one days you can double up chapters at the end of the month. And since Proverbs is not chronologically organized, you can jump in at any time.

Too many Christians shoot themselves in the foot by trying to go from not having *any* daily devotions at all to reading the Bible through in a year. That may work for a few, but most people will quickly find themselves sinking in spiritual quicksand.

Another reason this plan is so effective is that it is impossible to read a chapter in Proverbs and not walk away with at least one very practical principle you can "flesh out" that very day. The topics addressed in the book are too numerous to count, but include:

- Work ethics and lazy habits
- Wisdom and foolishness
- Family life and business practices
- Money management and the fear of the Lord
- Alcohol and lust
- Pleasant speech and pride

Each day try to remember just one principle from your reading. Write out the verse on a 3x5 card and carry it around that day. This will help you grow in wisdom and develop the lifestyle of being a doer of the Word and not a hearer only

(James 1:22). Now, in time you will want to move from Proverbs into other parts of the Bible, but if consistency is your struggle right now then I encourage you to use this plan for three months. Then add five psalms a day for another three months. By the end of six months you will have firmly established a new habit.

By the way, this doesn't work just for personal devotions. It is *perfect* for establishing the habit of family devotions—and what parent can give his child better wisdom than God's Word? Over the years I have seen many fathers find this suggestion just what they needed to begin family devotions for the first time or to get back on track if they have fallen into lazy habits. Try this approach for one year and see the "teaching moments" with your children abound!

CHAPTER THIRTY-NINE

Preparing for Sunday

Practical counsel for worshippers

In one Sunday evening sermon series I taught practical applications on the seriousness of corporate worship and the resulting preparation it should impress upon us. I received a great deal of positive feedback and was encouraged to include this material. So, here it is.

In reflecting on Hebrews 12:18–29, it is obvious that God considers corporate worship a serious matter, not the game the modern church often plays. Here's what it says:

> For you have not come to the mountain that may be touched and that burned with fire, and to blackness and darkness and tempest, and the sound of a trumpet and the voice of words, so that those who heard it begged that the word should not be spoken to them anymore. (For they could not endure what was commanded: "And if so much as a beast touches the mountain, it shall be stoned or shot with an arrow." And so terrifying was the sight

that Moses said, "I am exceedingly afraid and trembling." But you have come to Mount Zion and to the city of the living God, the heavenly Jerusalem, to an innumerable company of angels, to the general assembly and church of the firstborn who are registered in heaven, to God the Judge of all, to the spirits of just men made perfect, to Jesus the Mediator of the new covenant, and to the blood of sprinkling that speaks better things than that of Abel. See that you do not refuse Him who speaks. For if they did not escape who refused Him who spoke on earth, much more shall we not escape if we turn away from Him who speaks from heaven, whose voice then shook the earth; but now He has promised, saying, "Yet once more I shake not only the earth, but also heaven." Now this, "Yet once more," indicates the removal of those things that are being shaken, as of things that are made, that the things which cannot be shaken may remain. Therefore, since we are receiving a kingdom which cannot be shaken, let us have grace, by which we may serve God acceptably with reverence and godly fear. For our God is a consuming fire.

If God, Who is "a consuming fire," receives worship (indeed, *seeks* it; John 4:23) from sinners like you and me, should we not be more serious about how we approach Him? If worship demands reverence and awe, should we not *prepare ourselves* to meet our God? It is questions like these that led me to form the following suggestions in preparing for Sunday worship. I have included practical, mundane preparations that free up more time for personal, heart, and soul preparation. May the application of this counsel lead you into a deeper, more God-centered, and heartfelt worship experience.

I. Saturday Evening

A. Practical Preparations

1. Prepare Sunday's meals.
   a. Breakfast made and table set—simple, self-serve breakfasts, such as muffins or fruit bread, yogurt, hard-boiled eggs, etc.
   b. Noon meal planned and prepared, when possible.
2. Gas up the car (this was even more important when we lived forty minutes from church).
3. Pick out clothes and take care of needed ironing.
4. Find Bibles (and shoes!) and lay them out.
5. Set aside your offering (and help your children set aside theirs): "*So let each one give* as he purposes in his heart, not grudgingly or of necessity; for God loves a cheerful giver" (2 Corinthians 9:7).
6. Bible class teachers: make final lesson preparations.
7. Have children take baths.
8. Get to bed early.
   a. Avoid late-night Saturday activities as much as possible.
   b. Avoid television, video games, and fluffy books. Avoid anything that trivializes or tends to put your mind in neutral. God's thoughts are deep (Psalm 92:5).

The purpose of these practical preparations is to prevent potential distractions and decrease the tension-level in your home, which often results in irritations and conflicts.

B. Personal Preparations

1. Delight in the WORD.
   a. Read Psalm 32 or Psalm 51 and spend time in confession.
   b. Read some Scriptures about worship (e.g., John 4, Hebrews 12:18–29, Psalm 95–100).
   c. For Communion Sundays: read a Gospel account of the Crucifixion or Hebrews, chapters 7–10.
   d. For Communion Sundays: resolve interpersonal conflicts, seek forgiveness where needed (Matthew 5:23, 24; 1 Corinthians 11:17–34).
   e. Read a chapter from a solid devotional book, such as *The Knowledge of the Holy*, by A.W. Tozer. I define a devotional book as one that directs my thoughts to the character and works of God.

2. Devote yourself to prayer. Pray for:
   a. Worship service as a whole—that it would glorify God.
   b. Worship service participants.
   c. Ushers and greeters.
   d. Scripture readers.
   e. Musicians, choir, and songleaders.
   f. Preacher.
   g. Nursery workers.
   h. Bible class teachers.
   i. Visitors.
   j. Unbelievers who may be present.
   k. Bible class teachers: pray for your students and fellow teachers.

3. Discipline your mind with song:
   a. Fill the house with good, worshipful music.
   b. Sing some hymns aloud.

The purpose of these personal preparations is to sensitize your heart and mind to meet the Lord in corporate worship. The goal is to go to bed with the Lord in your thoughts.

II. Sunday Morning

A. Practical Preparations

1. Get up early.
2. Keep the television off (the latest news from CNN can wait).

B. Personal Preparations

1. The Word: read a Psalm or two.
2. Prayer
   a. Pray for yourself and your family.
   b. Pray for the worship service and all who will be present.
3. Song
   a. Use a tape or CD of hymns and praise songs as background music in your home.
   b. Listen to hymns and praise songs in the car on the way to church.
4. Get to church *at least* fifteen minutes before the service begins.
   a. Take care of miscellaneous details.
   b. Give a word of encouragement to at least one other person.
   c. Take babies to the nursery and have other children use the restrooms.

d. Be seated in the sanctuary. Spend time looking up songs and Scripture and/or pray for yourself and your fellow worshippers.

5. Worship the Lord with all your heart in the company of the redeemed! (Psalm 107:1, 2).

It is good to give thanks to the LORD, and to sing praises to Your name, O Most High; to declare Your lovingkindness in the morning, and Your faithfulness every night, on an instrument of ten strings, on the lute, and on the harp, with harmonious sound. For You, LORD, have made me glad through Your work; I will triumph in the works of Your hands. O LORD, how great are Your works! Your thoughts are very deep.

(Psalm 92:1–5)

CHAPTER FORTY

Freedom from the "Performance Treadmill"

Learning to live by grace

Ten years ago I received a book written by one of my favorite authors, Jerry Bridges. The book is entitled *Transforming Grace*.[61] I immediately read the first few chapters and set it aside for no memorable reason (Providence had another plan to use it later). There it sat until early this year, when I sensed a powerful working of the Spirit in my life bringing me to a "new," deeper understanding of God's grace.

I found myself constantly frustrated and, at times, depressed. I felt like a constant failure who could never measure up to my perfectionist expectations and, therefore, did not feel fully accepted by God. Oh, I knew I was born again. There was no question in my mind about that. But I found it almost impossible to simply rest in my acceptance with God. So, He sent Jerry Bridges to me as a faithful counselor to help me see the cause of my frustration: I had shifted the basis of my acceptance with God from His grace alone to His grace *plus* my daily performance for Him. The writer exposed my wrong thinking:

My observation of Christendom is that most of us tend to base our personal relationship with God on our performance instead of on His grace. If we've performed well—whatever "well" is in our opinion—then we expect God to bless us. If we haven't done so well, our expectations are reduced accordingly. In this sense, we live by works rather than grace. We are saved by grace, but we are living by the "sweat" of our own performance. (p. 1l, 12)

Can you relate? Even though you know in your head that your salvation was accomplished solely by the grace of God apart from your own works, do you sometimes wonder if God really accepts you? If you do not always "feel" accepted, it may be you have exchanged the security of your standing in Christ with the uncertainty of what Bridges calls "the performance treadmill" and, therefore, are not truly living by grace. Here's how he describes it:

Living by grace instead of by works means you are free from the performance treadmill. It means God has already given you an "A" when you deserved an "F." He has already given you a full day's pay even though you may have worked for only one hour. It means you don't have to perform certain spiritual disciplines to earn God's approval. Jesus Christ has already done that for you. You are loved and accepted by God through the merit of Jesus, and you are blessed by God through the merit of Jesus. Nothing you ever do will cause Him to love you any more or any less. He loves you strictly by His grace given to you through Jesus. (p. 73)

At the same time I was reading Bridges, God providentially led me to ask one of our missionary staff, Blaine Adamson, to teach the adult Bible class one Sunday morning.

Unbeknownst to me, he chose to teach from the first chapter of Ephesians—on how the grace of God is evidenced by the security of the believer's position in Christ. The apostle's point in the passage is that salvation is totally, "to the praise of the glory of His grace, by which *He has made us accepted in the Beloved*" (Ephesians 1:6). One sentence in Blaine's lesson jumped out, hit me upside the head, and firmly planted itself in my mind; hopefully, forever. He said: "God does not bless me according to my performance. Instead, I am already blessed in Christ." I *knew* that! I'd probably even *said* something at least remotely like it at one time or another, but I needed to *hear* it said in exactly that way for it to sink in—another affirmation of the Spirit of God renewing my mind.

Bridges said it this way:

> To live by grace is to live solely by the merit of Jesus Christ. To live by grace is to base my entire relationship with God, including my acceptance and standing with Him, on my union with Christ. It is to recognize that in myself I bring nothing of worth to my relationship with God, because even my righteous acts are like filthy rags in His sight (Isaiah 64:6). Even my best works are stained with motives and imperfect performance. I never truly love God with *all* my heart, and I never truly love my neighbor with the degree or consistency with which I love myself. (p. 101)

Therefore, if we base our favor with God on our performance, we will never truly think we are accepted, because all our past and present performances are flawed by our sin and the stubbornness of our depravity, and there will always be another performance ahead—a performance we *might* just fail. Instead, we must meditate on key passages of Scripture that assure us of our standing in grace:

> Therefore, having been justified by faith, we have peace with God through our Lord Jesus Christ, through whom also we have access by faith into this grace in which we stand, and rejoice in hope of the glory of God.
>
> (Romans 5:1, 2)

> For when we were still without strength, in due time Christ died for the ungodly. For scarcely for a righteous man will one die; yet perhaps for a good man someone would even dare to die. But God demonstrates His own love toward us, in that while we were still sinners, Christ died for us.
>
> (Romans 5:6–8)

> There is therefore now no condemnation for those who are in Christ Jesus.
>
> (Romans 8:1 NASB)

> For you did not receive the spirit of bondage again to fear, but you received the Spirit of adoption by whom we cry out, "Abba, Father." The Spirit Himself bears witness with our spirit that we are children of God.
>
> (Romans 8:15, 16)

As we meditate on truths like these, our minds are renewed and freed from enslavement to performance. Focusing on the truth that our acceptance with God is purely because of His grace toward us in Christ will keep us humble and dependent on the Spirit of God. Bridges ends his chapter on, "The Performance Treadmill," with an illustration of Mephibosheth, son of Jonathan (2 Samuel 9), in which he likens the lame man's ever-helpless physical condition to our spiritual need of grace and makes this application:

"Mephibosheth never got over his crippled condition. He never got to the place where he could leave the king's table and make it on his own. And neither do we" (p. 24).

That is the key! We must never lose sight of our helpless condition and desperate need of grace. As we make progress in the Christian life, we must guard against the pride that too often grows from valuing our performance above His grace. True acceptance is based solely on God's gracious work in Jesus. When we learn to rest in this truth, feelings of acceptance by God will follow.

> *Wonderful grace of Jesus, greater than all my sin;*
> *How shall my tongue describe it,*
> *Where shall its praise begin?*
> *Taking away my burden, setting my spirit free,*
> *For the wonderful grace of Jesus reaches me.*
>
> *Wonderful the matchless grace of Jesus,*
> *Deeper than the mighty rolling sea;*
> *Higher than the mountain, sparkling like a fountain,*
> *All sufficient grace for even me;*
> *Broader than the scope of my transgressions,*
> *Greater far than all my sin and shame;*
> *O magnify the precious name of Jesus,*
> *Praise His Name!*[62]

Endnotes

[1] James L. Snyder, Ed., *A.W. Tozer on Worship and Entertainment* (Camp Hill, PA: Christian Publications, 1997), p. 175.

[2] Charles H. Spurgeon, *The Treasury of David – Volume 1a* (Grand Rapids, MI: Zondervan, 1977), p. 2.

[3] *Grace Greater Than Our Sin*, text by Julia H. Johnston, verse 2.

[4] Glenda Revell, *Glenda's Story* (Lincoln, NE: Gateway to Joy, 1994). This wonderful little book is still available from Back to the Bible ministries, at 1-800-811-2397, or www.backtothebible.org.

[5] William MacDonald, *Believer's Bible Commentary* (Nashville, TN: Thomas Nelson, 1995), p. 2078.

[6] Ed Bulkley, *Why Christians Can't Trust Psychology* (Eugene, OR: Harvest House, 1993), p. 122.

[7] *The Old Rugged Cross*, George Bennard, 1873-1958.

[8] Arthur Bennett, Editor., *The Valley of Vision* (Great Britain: Banner of Truth Trust, 2003, orig. 1975), p. 14.

[9] Douglas Wilson, *The Case for Classical Christian Education* (Wheaton, IL: Crossway Books, 2003), pp. 47, 48.

[10] *Vine's Complete Expository Dictionary of Old and New Testament Words* (Nashville, TN: Thomas Nelson, 1985), p. 204.

[11] Ray C. Stedman, *Is This All There Is to Life?* (Grand Rapids, MI: Discovery House Publishers, 1999), p. 64.

[12] Gracia Burnham with Dean Merrill, *In the Presence of My Enemies* (Wheaton, IL: Tyndale House, 2003).

[13] John MacArthur and Wayne Mack, eds., *Introduction to Biblical Counseling* (Dallas, TX: Word, 1994), p. 44.

[14] *Introduction to Biblical Counseling*, p. 45.

[15] *Introduction to Biblical Counseling*, p. 4.

[16] Jay E. Adams, *Competent to Counsel* (Grand Rapids: Zondervan, 1970), pp. 44, 45, 49, 50.

[17] Kenneth S. Wuest, *Wuest's Word Studies: First Peter in the Greek NT* (Grand Rapids: Eerdmans, 1942), p. 25

[18] Ibid., p. 27.

[19] Bryan Clark, *All It's meant to Be,* (Lincoln, NE: Back to the Bible Publishers, 2000)

[20] R. Kent Hughes, *Disciplines of a Godly Man* (Wheaton, IL: Crossway Books, 1991), p. 73. I have used this outstanding book in discipling men for many years. The chapter containing this comment, "Discipline of the Mind," is more than worth the price of the book.

[21] Thomas Watson, *The Doctrine of Repentance* (Great Britain: Banner of Truth, 1987, orig. 1668), p. 24.

[22] *The New Hampshire Confession of Faith*, 1833.

[23] *Vine's Complete Expository Dictionary of Old and New Testament Words* (Nashville, TN: Thomas Nelson, 1985), pp. 525, 526.

24 Wayne Grudem, *Systematic Theology* (Great Britain: Inter-Varsity Press and Grand Rapids: Zondervan, 1994), p. 13.

25 Thomas Watson, *The Doctrine of Repentance* (Great Britain: Banner of Truth, 1987, orig. 1668).

26 Charles A. Tindly, 1851–1933. Copyright: Singspiration, 1968.

27 Kurt Kaiser (Word Music, 1975), Verses. 1, 2. Paul Tautges, Verse 3.

28 Walter C. Kaiser, *Hard Saying of the Old Testament* (Downers Grove, IL: Inter-Varsity Press), pp. 114, 115.

29 For an excellent discussion of this principle see, Kent and Barbara Hughes, *Liberating Ministry from the Success Syndrome* (Wheaton: Tyndale House Publishers, 1988), especially pp. 35,43.

30 John Piper, *A Godward Life* (Sisters, OR: Multnomah Press, 1997.), pp. 28–29.

31 Charles Dickens, *A Christmas Carol and Other Christmas Writings* (London, England: Penguin Classics, 2003 edition).

32 *John G. Paton: Missionary to the New Hebrides, An Autobiography Edited by His Brother James Paton* (Edinburgh: The Banner of Truth Trust, 1965, orig. 1889, 1891), pp. 372–374.

33 Douglas Wilson, *The Case for Classical Christian Education* (Wheaton, IL: Crossway Books, 2003), p. 20.

34 Wilson, pp. 17, 18.

35 Sworn affidavit, 22 January, 2003, State of New York. A copy of the complete affidavit can be printed from the "Resources" page at www.returntotheword.org.

[36] Quoted by Robert D. Smith, M.D., *The Christian Counselor's Medical Desk Reference* (Stanley, NC: Timeless Texts, 2000), p. 145.

[37] Edward T. Welch, *Blame It on the Brain?* (Phillipsburg, NJ: P&R Publishing, 1998), p. 142.

[38] Robert D. Smith, M.D., *The Christian Counselor's Medical Desk Reference* (Stanley, NC: Timeless Texts, 2000), p. 148.

[39] Welch, p. 137.

[40] Smith, p. 149.

[41] David Powlison, *Seeing With New Eyes* (Phillipsburg, NJ: P&R Publishing, 2003), p. 243.

[42] I credit this thought to Dr. Hubert Hartzler, one of my professors at Calvary Bible College, who influenced me more than he realizes.

[43] Thomas Brooks, from a sermon entitled: "Are We Mad Now to Pursue After Holiness?" Published in the *Free Grace Broadcaster* (Pensacola, FL: a ministry of Mt. Zion Bible Church, Fall 2003), pp. 25–49.

[44] John Bunyan, *Grace Abounding to the Chief of Sinners* (New Kensington, PA: Whitaker House, 1993), pp. 183, 184.

[45] Brooks, p. 29.

[46] Eric Schlosser, *Fast Food Nation: The Dark Side of the All-American Meal* (New York: Houghton Mifflin, 2001), pp. 240–242.

[47] *The Works of Jonathan Edwards, Volume 1* (Great Britain: Banner of Truth Trust, 1995; orig. 1834), p. xxxv.

[48] Rus Walton, *Biblical Solutions to Contemporary Problems* (Brentwood, TN: Wolgemuth & Hyatt), p. 285.

[49] Edward T. Welch, *Homosexuality: Speaking the Truth in Love* (Phillipsburg, NJ: P&R Publishing, 2000), p. 37.

[50] Joe Dallas, *Desires in Conflict* (Eugene, OR: Harvest House, 1991), p. 92.

[51] Welch, pp. 14, 19.

[52] John Jefferson Davis, *Evangelical Ethics* (Phillipsburg, NJ: Presbyterian & Reformed Publishing, 1985).

[53] R. Kent Hughes, *Disciplines of a Godly Man* (Wheaton, IL: Crossway Books, 1991).

[54] *Webster's New World Dictionary – Second College Edition* (New York: Simon & Schuster, 1970).

[55] Watson, p. 37.

[56] Hughes, p. 133.

[57] www.nife.gov

[58] Bernard Ruffin, *Fanny Crosby, Hymn Writer* (Uhrichsville, OH: Barbour Publishing, Inc., 1995), pp. 6, 7.

[59] Kenneth W. Osbeck, *101 More Hymn Stories* (Grand Rapids, MI: Kregel Publications, 1985), p. 237.

[60] All page references in the text refer to *Fanny Crosby: An Autobiography* (Grand Rapids, Baker Book House, 1986, orig. 1906 by James H. Earle and Company under the title *Memories of Eighty Years*).

[61] Jerry Bridges, *Transforming Grace* (Colorado Springs, CO: NavPress, 1991).

[62] *Wonderful Grace of Jesus*, Haldor Lillenas, 1885-1959.

To order additional copies of

Have your credit card ready and call:

1-877-421-READ (7323)

or please visit our web site at
www.pleasantword.com

Also available at:
www.amazon.com
and
www.barnesandnoble.com

.

Printed in the United States
60155LVS00002B/58-78